It's an Ill Wind, Indeed…
that blows no good

A Memoir

By Joan Callaway

D0747362

It's an Ill Wind, Indeed...

that blows no good

By Joan Callaway

Copyright 2011 by Joan Callaway

ISBN: 13-978-1466215214

Printed in the United States

1. Grief   2. Bereavement.   3. Adolescent grief.   4. Loss of a child..
5.Sudden death 6 Unresolved grief. 7. Renew and rebuild after loss.

Dedication

To my fellow memoir writers, whose optimism and feedback have kept me writing…

To my children and grandchildren for who they are now and who they will become…

To Ed Callaway, my husband and best friend, who gave me the confidence and courage to live and love again. I feel fortunate beyond words to share my life with you.

Acknowledgments

Thanks to my parents who instilled in me the belief that I could do anything if I just had the will. To my mother, particularly, for her example of resiliency and entrepreneurship. To my grandmother who told me many times, "It's an Ill wind, indeed, Joni, that blows no good."

To my children, Valerie, Marci, Laurie and Mark, who gave my life meaning and purpose, for their willingness to let their stories be told. To the inspirational words of George Bernard Shaw, who said, "This is the true joy in life….My life belongs to the whole community, and as long as I live, it is my privilege to do for it whatever I can."

To Pat Hutchinson who years ago invited me to join the writing group to which she belonged. To the memory of Dorothy Dunning who encouraged me to write about the most painful experience of my life. To my writing group friends, who listened patiently, gave welcome advice, and kept my hands moving across the keys, page by page, chapter by chapter.

My heartfelt thanks to all those, seen and unseen, who stood by our family during our darkest hours and for years beyond. To Shipley Walters – thank you for talking me through my disconsolate days. To Joyce Wisner and all the friends of my teenagers, who so often comforted my soul and made me laugh. To Nancy Keltner for her continual optimism and enthusiasm. Our friendship is one of my life's great treasures.

And finally, to Ed, a special husband and friend, who has over the years suffered with me, cried with me, and laughed with me, and who helped me in those early years work through my grief.

Contents

Preface

Wisdom arrives through a childlike sense of wonder, or through "centering." Within us lives a merciful being who helps us to our feet however many times we fall.
-M. C. Richards

"All beginnings are difficult." These words from the Talmud – such simple words of wisdom – certainly apply to this story of my life as I struggle with what to write and realize that *whatever* I write are only *my* truths, *my* perceptions. The events and interchanges related in this book are as I recall them and may not be remembered in this same way by family members and friends who read this book, nor might they have been by those who, sadly, are no longer around to comment or contradict.

I have been as honest and forthright as possible and have contributed as much of emotional significance of my life as I can recollect. It is through this truth-telling of my life that those who have shared my life and those who come after may know me a little better and perhaps profit from the lessons I have learned. As Russell Baker wrote in his memoirs: *"We all come from the past, and children ought to know what it was that went into their making."*

Each of the beginnings of my life seems to have involved a turning point - a loss and then growth. I received a quote at the major turning point of my life, which resonated with me: *"Our only security in life is our ability to change."* I have had many opportunities to test this theory as I have recalled and written the following stories from my life. I finally arrived at the emotional truth that while I may not have had any control over what happened in life, I did have the freedom to choose my attitude in any set of circumstances, the freedom to choose how I thought about things. This realization has over the years helped me to make subsequent endings and new beginnings far less challenging. When I altered the wording of the quote just a bit to read: "ability to adapt," I found that it worked for every new beginning of my life.

I wrote this book as a part of my life story - the last forty years - for my children and grandchildren. It's their story, too - a story about learning to live again – to love again - after a severe and sudden loss. I started out writing about my birth, mother, father, and siblings, chronologically. That seemed logical to my linear mind. But my psyche had a different idea – this story begged - demanded - to be told, before I could put pen to those earlier days.

This is the story of my climb out of the abyss after the sudden death and loss of my husband and young son through a fire in our home – a story of the survival, coping, and eventual healing of the whole family. Many have said they don't know how one stays sane in the face of such tragedy. That's the reason I wrote the book. I'm here to tell you that one can stay mostly sane most of the time, survive, and eventually come out the other side. Although death ends a life, it never ends a relationship. Even after such a long time, I still have those little memorial services in my mind from time to time; a favorite song or some other trigger seemingly lies in wait to ambush my heartstrings. This book is my thank you to all those who helped me through my darkest days. If, in addition, the words in this book can make even one person's journey through grief a little easier, it will have been more than worth the effort.

Prologue

Winds of Change

Everywhere stillness, yet in this abeyance: seeds of change and new beginnings near.
                                        -Rainer Maria Rilke

December 31, 1970 (with literary liberties taken)

I always feel a bit melancholy toward the end of a vacation. The thought of preparing to leave our rented cabin at Soda Springs proved to be no different this time. We saw a casino show, visited with friends, and Glen and the kids skied in fresh powder every day. As usual, I preferred the warmth of the ski lodge, taking advantage of the opportunity to read a good book or do some writing. Although I never minded occasionally being interrupted to dole out a cup of hot chocolate when one of the family came in for a visit or to warm up by the fire.

Alas! Monday we have to return to our familiar schedules of work and school.

On what was to be our last full day of vacation, we all stomped the snow off our boots before storing them and the rest of our gear in the mud-room as we entered the chalet. Looking wind-burned, a smiling Glen joshed with Laurie, the middle of our five children, and said, "What a couple of hot dogs you guys are! I can't keep up with you anymore."

"Oh, you're not so bad yourself, Dad," the graceful, lithe Laurie replied.

"I was surprised. The lift line waits weren't nearly as long as I expected on a holiday. "

"Guess a lot of people stayed home to watch the Rose Bowl game."

Mark, who had made a beeline for the TV, still wearing his ski pants and sweater, chimed in, "Yeah, we were really lucky. Great skiing today! But the weather guy says a blizzard's on the way by tomorrow afternoon."

Overhearing that last comment of Mark's, I suggested that maybe we should pack up and head home.

"Not a bad idea," Glen replied and added, "But not tonight. Let's go tomorrow. We'll still beat the holiday traffic. We'll miss a day of skiing, but to be honest, I wouldn't mind an extra day at home before I have to go back to work. "

"Let's pack up as much as we can tonight and get an early start tomorrow." I agreed because I had to go back to work on Monday, as well. We had barely unpacked from a Christmas family reunion at my sister's home in Gold Beach, Oregon, when it had been time to repack for our trip to Tahoe. Our tree hadn't even been taken down yet.

"I'll call Valerie and let her know we'll be home tomorrow." The eldest of our three daughters, who was home from college on winter break, had stayed home with our younger son, Keith.

"Yeah! Give her and Keith a chance to clean up the house from the party they probably had," deadpanned Laurie. Ironic, because we all knew that Valerie was the least likely of our five children to throw a party in our absence.

"I'd better phone Marci over at the McCorkle cabin to tell her we're going home early. I'm assuming Marci will want to stay and ride home with them."

"Oh, d'ya think?" Laurie sneered, "Or maybe she'll say, 'Oh, Mom, of course, I want to give up some of the best skiing of the season to drive home with you guys.'"

Mark, the tease of the family, rolled his eyes and in a high falsetto imitation of his older sister's voice he added his two cents worth, "I'd especially like to come over and help clean bathrooms and haul stuff to the car through the snow." And then in his own voice, he added, "Yeah, sure!"

As I suspected, and as Mark and Laurie predicted, Marci elected to stay and enjoy another day on the slopes with Tim, her boyfriend for the better part of four years - since ninth grade at Emerson Junior High. The McCorkle's treated her almost like family.

The next day it was nearly three o'clock by the time we cleaned the cabin and loaded the car. As we hit the road a light dusting of fresh snow covered the car, and flurries were coming down hard by the time we reached the main road. Traffic seemed heavy for a Saturday, and it wasn't long before we came to a dead stop for nearly half an hour.

"There must be an accident way up ahead. I may as well put the chains on now, since we're stopped anyway," Glen said as he began to maneuver the car off the highway.

A few minutes later, "Do we have any Band-Aids?" he asked, as he slid his almost six foot athletic frame back into the driver's seat, just in time to move into the line of cars beginning to snake along. "I

2

scraped my knuckles getting those damned chains on." His brown hair was covered in white from the fresh fallen snow.

I had no trouble locating the bright blue First Aid kit we kept in the glove compartment for just such emergencies.

After a few miles of stops and starts, with badgering and bantering from the back seat, since Mark's gangly arms and legs never seemed to be in a place Laurie could tolerate, I said, "Let's sing!" After leading us in all the verses of Clementine, Glen stopped singing and concentrated on the traffic ahead.

At one of the longer stops, Mark and Laurie leaped out of the car to stretch their legs and peer up ahead to see what they could see. The new fallen snow proved too great a temptation for them and snowballs began to fly. The friendly battle provided an outlet for the pent-up aggression of a long car ride, until Glen tapped the horn when he noticed cars far ahead beginning to inch forward. The kids hopped in just in time for us to join the traffic toward Sacramento.

Both Mark, at thirteen and a half, who was rapidly transitioning into a rich bass-baritone, and Laurie, an alto, were members of their schools' choirs. The kids and I tried harmonizing a few verses of You Are My Sunshine. I soon grew tired, but Laurie and Mark continued singing in their inimitable version of Cockney accents Consider Yourself, a favorite song from the Broadway hit *Oliver.*

When things got quieter in the back seat, I leaned against the passenger window and dozed off, not waking until we turned off at the Russell Boulevard exit in Davis. Instead of the usual three hours, the trip took a little over five.

"I don't envy the McCorkle's drive home tomorrow," I said as we turned onto Mulberry Lane.

"Tomorrow I-80 will probably be a parking lot!" Glen agreed, and added, "And if this storm keeps up, it'll be miserable."

Arriving at our house at last, Mark and Laurie each grabbed a duffel bag. Between the four of us, we unloaded the Chevy station wagon in record time. "Let's leave the unpacking for tomorrow," I suggested.

"No argument from me," Glen said, tired from the drawn out drive home. He dropped all that he carried by the side of the family room where Valerie sat watching TV. "Hey, Val, how's it goin? Where's Keith?"

"He's in bed – asleep, I think. He crashed early."

"How'd you do on your Humanities paper?" I asked.

"I'm almost finished. Just a bit of polishing left to do. It'll feel so good to have it done when I go back to school. It's bad enough to have finals hanging over my head without a paper due, too."

3

"Your Mom and I remember what that was like. Whose bright idea was it anyway to have the semester end right after Christmas? It meant we always had to spend the whole vacation writing papers, reading, and looking over old lecture notes as we prepped for finals – or at least worried about it while we procrastinated."

"Yeah, Dad, but on the other hand, it does give you time to catch up on all the stuff you didn't get done during the semester."

"Well, I'm glad you got something accomplished. We sure appreciate your staying home and taking care of Keith this weekend. We owe you."

"Actually, it was kind of fun. We had an okay weekend, once Keith got through whining about not being able to go skiing, cause that 'clumsy, out-of-control, dumb ol' lady' plowed into him and dislocated his hip. I appeased him by taking him to Fluffy Donuts this morning and to the movies this afternoon. We went to the Grad for burgers and fries tonight."

"Not a bad consolation prize. Well, see you in the morning. I may even sleep in," Glen said as he headed for bed with a book.

Laurie and Mark stretched out on the floor in front of the couch with Val to watch the rest of The Partridge Family. I went down to peek in on Keith, who lay on his twin bed, only half-covered. When I went to pull the blanket up over him, I noticed that he wasn't in his pajamas. Silly boy! He was still wearing the tee shirt and jeans he had probably worn all day.

He had just celebrated his twelfth birthday on the twenty-ninth of December. A month earlier, as he had approached what we considered to be a responsible age, we had allowed him to get an early morning paper route. He was so proud - "At last, REAL money of my own."

On the day we left for Tahoe, he'd grumbled at first about how the orthopedist had told him he couldn't ski for another couple of weeks. He reconciled himself at last, though, chuckling, "I'll stay home with Val. It'll give me time to enjoy my new Christmas and birthday stuff...without Maaark. And anyway, I've got responsibilities," he said, with strong emphasis on the 're' and 'bil'.

Probably the reason he's still wearing his jeans. He's no doubt thinking how much time he'll save when he gets up at 5 a.m. to deliver his papers. Oh well, won't hurt him, I guess. Hope he brushed his teeth. Well, I'd better brush mine and get to bed...morning's not too far off.

The wind seemed to have picked up. I could hear it gusting through the trees outside our bedroom window. I nuzzled up close to Glen, who put down his book and cuddled back. "It's good to be home," he said.

"And snug in our own bed - together," I added. "I'm glad the work on the ten-year plan is finished. We've all missed this kind of weekend the past few months."

"I've missed them, too. Now I just have to get caught up on everything at work, and we'll be able to get back to normal."

It was not long before I heard him breathe deeply. Having slept for a good part of the drive home, I lay awake thinking back over the past twenty years of our marriage.

I miss him when he's away, and so do the kids. He is our anchor – and my rudder, too. He provides a stabilizing influence, especially on those days when I'm feeling under-slept and overextended.

For over two months, this late fall, he was on-loan from the University of California Davis Medical School to the President's Office of the University of California in Berkeley to work on a ten-year plan for health sciences. He slept in a motel and ate in restaurants near the UC Berkeley campus, coming to Davis only on an occasional weekend. Now that the project was finished, hopefully he would be home for good.

♠

I remembered then how our family decided to take up skiing. With the five gregarious children going in all directions, it had almost seemed we were losing our family - or at least our family's special time together. After we'd been in Davis a couple of years, Glen and I strategized: "The only way we are going to preserve any semblance of family is to find some activity that nobody will want to miss."

Many of their avid-skier friends headed for Tahoe every weekend during the winter, so skiing seemed like it might be the perfect solution for our family, too. And it has been. Our station wagon has memorized the way to all our favorite slopes. This weekend was a warm, wonderful family time, except for Val and Keith. And Val said that even she and Keith had some good alone time.

We had moved to Davis from New Orleans when Glen, trained as a hospital administrator, was hired four years ago as

5

Assistant Dean for Administration of the embryonic University of California Davis Medical School. Back on the West Coast, we were thrilled to be close to everything we loved about California -the Bay Area, the ocean, and especially the mountains. We felt lucky to have found a comfortable, if not perfect, home, as housing was at a premium in Davis in those days...especially for a family of seven!

Originally a three-bedroom one-story tract house with a rather small living room, the Cornelius house featured a wonderful "Great Room," perfect for our family's casual entertaining style and a house full of teenagers.

I remember thinking, as we did the walk-through with the realtor: It will do, but where will we put our formal dining set with china closet and buffet...and the baby grand piano? Where will everyone sleep?

Fortunately for us, the owners had converted the two-car garage into two bedroom-sized rooms, a laundry room, and an additional bath. The remodel included a small gas wall heater between what we thought we would likely use as two bedrooms.

I find it interesting that every resold house in Davis is still known by the name of the first owner...this one is the Cornelius House. I wonder how long that will go on. Will it ever become known as the Snodgrass House?

We arrived in Davis during the summer, so it took a while for the kids to settle into new schools and the neighborhood, but they were all adventuresome and gregarious. It wasn't long before they were going in all directions: Little League, swim team, cheerleading, dance classes, piano lessons, gymnastics, roller skating, bowling, as well as overnights with friends. "I'm beginning to think we need one of those microwave ovens to reheat all the dinners the kids are missing," I remember saying to Glen. "Either that or maybe we should start having mandatory mealtime attendance."

It's good to have Glen home again. I can cope when he's away on those extended assignments, but nobody says I have to like it. We've been in Davis since 1966. Imagine, four and a half years! – That's as long as we've lived in any one place in the almost twenty years we've been married. Though I must say, ever since Glen's been in Berkeley, I've had this eerie feeling that a change will be coming soon. We've put down roots here; I dread the thought of another move.

6

At a stop, visiting family in Gold Beach, Oregon, Glen, Me with Keith, Val; atop the station wagon: Marci, Laurie and Mark.

An Ill Wind Doth Blow

New Years Day, 1971

I became who I am on this day just weeks before my 40th birthday. I remember the precise moment.

"Mom, Dad, there's a fire!" Mark shouted as he ran down the hall toward our bedroom. "It's in Keith's room."

Glen catapulted from bed the minute he heard Mark's voice and hit the floor running. I grabbed my robe, shouting to anyone within hearing distance to get out of the house. I headed into the kitchen in time to get a glimpse of Glen's nude backside as he dashed from Keith's bedroom out towards the back yard through the utility room door. I could hear the crackling of flames and could smell and taste the acrid smoke billowing out from the same direction. I caught a glimpse of Laurie as she followed her dad out through the laundry room door.

I quickly dialed the Operator for help, simultaneously re-ordering Mark and Valerie to get out to the front lawn, along with Roby, our Keeshond, while giving our address to the dispatcher with, "Yes, everyone is out!" before running out the front door.

As soon as I dialed I remembered that one is not supposed to make a phone call from a burning house, but at the time, I didn't think; I just did it automatically.

Relieved that everyone was safe, I collapsed on the front lawn, shivering and huddled in the bitter cold wind, horrorstruck as I sat and watched the flames lick through the roof above Keith's bedroom.

Laurie yelled to me from the corner of the house, "Mom, Keith's still in the house! Dad needs help!"

I found my feet and ran, before I had a chance to think of more than, Oh, my God! I told the fire department everyone was out! What if we can't get him out? Incredulous, as if moving in a nightmare, I ran to the side of the house to join the effort to rescue Keith.

I was confused in the split second it took to think a thought: When I saw Glen running out of the laundry room door, he was alone! He must have been repelled by the flames and all of that smoke. Then when he was unable to get into Keith's room because of flames, he must have come around here to break a window. The glass lay shattered at our bare feet. Glen gasped for breath and, for some reason, unfathomable to me at the time, he couldn't seem able to lift Keith out through the high overhead window.

If Glen, strong as he is, can't get him out, how will I be able to lift him down? I wondered, and then thought, "Thank, God! I hear the fire trucks!"

The window presented an awkward position for my five-foot-five frame, but with what must have been a boost of adrenaline Laurie and I finally pulled Keith to safety. My stomach felt queasy at the touch of his jeans, scorched and crumbling beneath my fingers, as I carried him out onto the front lawn.

I remembered then that he'd slept in his clothes last night, because he had probably thought it would expedite his delivery of the early morning Sacramento Bee. He won't be delivering papers this morning, I thought as I placed him carefully onto the ground.

My usually so in-charge and capable husband staggered away from the house, and collapsed on the damp lawn a few feet away. Keith was crying quietly, "Mom, it hurts."

"I know it does, honey. It'll be okay. Help is on the way."

Although it seemed like a lifetime, as I watched our lives pass before my eyes, all that thinking probably took only seconds before the fire trucks arrived. That time I was sure when I told the firemen there was no one left in the house.

Glen lay stretched out on the lawn, gasping for air, while Keith lay at my side, no longer crying. Two firemen came to administer oxygen and assess their injuries.

"Where's Marci?" a neighbor asked anxiously, as she started to lead the shivering teenagers across the street to her home.

Laurie interrupted her crying long enough to answer. "She's not here. She stayed up in the mountains with McCorkle's."

I watched the fire hoses roll out from the trucks and play water on the flames shooting through the roof of our one-story home, silently grateful for the ugly hydrant that plagued our landscaping efforts.

Oblivious, in the dark, that Glen was even injured, I turned toward his prostrate body and asked, "Where shall we have them take Keith, Hon?" It was then I heard a third fireman radio for two ambulances to be dispatched – my first inkling that two ambulances would be needed. Until then, it hadn't occurred to me that Glen would also need to be taken to an emergency room for treatment. It was only when he didn't answer that I realized he now lay unconscious under the dark early morning skies, the only light coming from the ignited house and a distant street lamp. "Take them to the Sacramento

Medical Center," I said, certain it would be the best place for them to get emergency care for the kind of injuries I knew Keith had sustained. At the time, I hadn't realized the extent of Glen's injuries.

"Sorry, Ma'am. They'll have to be taken to the nearest hospital. That's Davis Community Hospital. "

Community? That's just a small rural hospital out in the cornfields. It's only staffed with nurses at night. There's no one there to take care of any but the simplest of emergencies, [As I write this, we are lucky that Davis now has a full-service hospital with an efficient and qualified E.R. – Sutter Davis Hospital.]

Ambulances screamed up. As they loaded the gurneys, I renewed my pleas through sobs, "Please take them to the UC Med Center. There's no house staff out at Community. It'll take another twenty minutes to get an on-call doctor out there. Oh, please. They'll get emergency burn treatment faster at the Med Center."

"It's the law, Ma'am. We have to take them to the nearest hospital. Sorry," as they rolled the gurney carrying Keith toward the first ambulance.

I followed, resigned, but shouted a last minute plea to Valerie. "Call Dean Tupper. Tell him what happened. Tell him we're going out to Community Hospital, but that I'm sure Keith will have to be transferred to the Med Center as soon as a doctor gets there."

'Tup' will help. He'll arrange to have specialists waiting at the Med Center by the time we get there. I just know that Keith will need a lot of special treatment before this is over. And God only knows about Glen. They say he's unconscious. I wonder why that is. He wasn't in the fire. Was he?

I rambled in my head, frantic: A trip out to community hospital - ten minutes at least. Another fifteen minutes until a doctor can get there. Maybe they've already called ahead. Oh, Damn! We could have been at the Med Center in the time all this is taking. I hope these two ambulances hang around until the doctor issues the orders to transfer them. I'm positive they'll be needed. Oh, I wish Glen would wake up and tell me what to do. Wake up? What am I thinking? They say he's unconscious - not asleep!

By the time I settled in beside Keith in the first of the two ambulances, I became aware he had lost consciousness, too. Scary as that was, I felt relief that he could no longer feel the pain.

Sirens always sound eerie as they pass by on adjacent streets, but the sound does not compare with that inside the vehicle. Aware of the intermittent flashing of red lights, I shuddered at the shrill wail reverberating off the walls at the back of the ambulance in which Keith and I rode. I chilled at the echoing high-pitched sound from the one behind us that carried Glen.

One of the ambulance emergency attendants apologized, telling me en route to the hospital that if I had called the ambulances myself they could have followed my instructions, but since the fire department summoned them, the law required they be taken to the nearest ER.

This can't really be happening – it's a bad dream.

In the next part of the living nightmare, a nurse ushered me into the admitting office of our small community hospital as the attendants unloaded the ambulances. The nurse started with, "I need to have you sign this consent form," and then the ubiquitous: "Do you have insurance?"

I advised her through tears and obvious angst what she already must have known: "Yes, we have Blue Cross, but I'm sorry, I don't have my purse or any insurance information. There was a fire at my house. Please just get some doctors here." And then at the next question, irritated now, I said, "Don't worry. You'll get your money." She must have realized I was about to explode, because she gave up her questioning and shuffled me off to chairs outside the emergency room. I protested and said, "I don't want to sit out here. I need to be with my husband and son."

"I know, but I'm sorry. You can't go in there. Just wait here. Someone will come out soon and tell you how they're doing." Her words of comfort came a bit late from my perspective: "Everything is being done that can be done."

I've never felt so helpless and alone. What's happening in there?

To my relief, minutes later Mary and John Tupper came through the door. Mary rushed over and put her arms around me. Tup tried to reassure me, "I called Jack Benner. He's getting a team organized at the Med Center. They'll be ready and waiting when the ambulances arrive." Although he didn't have privileges at this hospital, he went through the doors of the Emergency Room to see how Glen and Keith were doing.

I became more and more frightened as I heard snatches of conversation from inside the ER: "He stopped breathing - ...resuscitation...tracheotomy?"

Who stopped breathing?" I wondered to Mary. "Tracheotomy? That means serious trouble with breathing. Who stopped breathing?" I asked in a state of panic.

Glen seemed to be gasping for breath back there on the lawn. Tracheotomy? What does that mean? Maybe he inhaled some smoke. It may have caused some swelling in his throat. Perhaps it's a good thing we came to this little hospital after all.

In what seemed like forever, but was really not more a few minutes, Tup came out of the Emergency Room and told us, "They're being transferred over to the Med Center. They're loading them into the ambulances now."

"Can I go with them?" I asked.

"No, Joni, it'll be better if we drive you over. You won't be able to see them for awhile anyway. While they're getting settled in and evaluated by the specialists, we'll find you some clothes to wear."

I haven't even noticed that I am still in my robe and barefoot. Clothes? Do I even have any? The kids...

"Oh, I can't even imagine how frantic the kids must be! Somehow we've got to warn Marci, too. She's still up in the mountains. She'll be coming home later today with the McCorkle's. I don't want her to hear about it on the radio – or on TV. I don't want her to arrive home to that house. I have no idea how we can reach her," an articulation of a jumble of thoughts tore through my shattered mind, one after another, and all at once. "I should call Glen's mother – and mine, too."

Telephone numbers? My mind – it's playing tricks on me. I can't think straight. I don't remember a single phone number. We'll have to call Information, I guess. But I want to go over to the Med Center.

"They will be okay, won't they, Tup?"

My Foxhole

A bit of amnesia is a good thing. The mind must have a way of protecting itself during such a time as this; there must be some mechanism that dulls the memory of such anguish.

I have little knowledge of what happened in the next few hours after the ambulances left for Sacramento; I have no recollection of conversations with the kids or where the kids and I got the clothes we wore for the next few days. Laurie recalls that the older daughter of a neighbor thoughtfully brought some clothing, along with some rather mature sexy bras, which she says, "offered us a brief respite of bemused, surprised laughter." I do know that our every need was met, except for what we wanted most: for someone to tell us that Glen and Keith were going to be all right. Laurie and I were even numb to the fact that our hands were slightly burned until a doctor, who stopped by to visit, noticed and offered to treat them for us.

Our good friend, Dr. Jack Benner, an internist, oversaw the care of Glen and Keith. He met with me when I arrived at the hospital and forewarned me of what I would see when I entered Glen and Keith's rooms, but nothing could have prepared me. I had never before seen a burn patient.

On walking into Keith's intensive care room, I felt a surge of pain so profound I could scarcely breathe. I couldn't so much as hold his hand with all of those tubes delivering fluid and oxygen to his swollen reddened body for fear my touch would hurt him. I whispered to him and then shouted when the nurses suggested that it might rouse him from his coma. Blessedly though, he never woke to feel what would have been excruciating pain or to hear me say words that in my heart I would have known to be lies.

To my shame, I am relieved.

I began to absorb that if Keith survived, it would be a prolonged rehabilitation; someone told me that patients with burns of this severity were transferred to a burn center in Texas for long-term treatment. I tried to think otherwise, but in my heart I knew it unlikely he would ever again be the active, funny, fun-loving little boy we had known. I could no longer deny what deep down I knew to be true.

I didn't think Glen was burned – not like Keith. He hadn't really gone into the burning room – had he? His seemed to me to just be a breathing problem from too much smoke...wasn't it?. I was able to talk to him when he regained consciousness. His first word through the 'trach tube' was a one-word question, "Keith?"

"You saved him, Hon," not wanting him to know how badly burned Keith was and how grave his condition. "You just rest and get well. We love you so much. We need you."

He spoke briefly through his swollen eyes, sending a clear message to Jack to take care of us. I never asked if the children could visit; I couldn't bear the thought of them seeing their father and brother in their conditions -- unrecognizable.

As we left Glen's room, I looked to Jack for verification that Glen really had saved Keith: "Keith will be okay, won't he, Jack?"

And then I knew. I could tell by the look on his face and by the tone of his voice that there was little hope for Keith. When he said, "Joni, I just hope to hell we can save Glen!" I began to comprehend for the first time that there was a question as to Glen's survival, as well.

At about 6 a.m., the number of the McCorkle cabin where Marci was staying was located. Chet McCorkle immediately woke everyone and just told them, "We have to go back to Davis right now," without giving them any reason. "Marci, get your things together. You'll ride with me. Tim, you go with your mother. We'll see you back in Davis."

Without stopping for anything, they left. As Marci relates it, "We knew something was wrong, but he didn't tell us what. He finally told me what had happened just before we got to the hospital. When we got off the elevator on the burn unit floor, someone – I didn't know who it was – met us and blurted out to Chet, whom he apparently knew, 'It doesn't look like they're going to make it.' And then, finally realizing who I must be, turned to me and said, "Your mom doesn't want you to see them."

It haunts me that Marci had to learn about it in this way.

I was torn between wanting to be at the hospital, to be there when Keith woke up, and being at "home" with our teenagers who I knew needed my support. I shuttled back and forth in the cars of friends, who wisely were afraid to let me drive.

How can I give support to anyone right now? I'm barely able to keep it together myself.

I found the things Dr. Benner and the resident had said so disturbing that once I absorbed it, I pushed it to the back of my mind – denial. The idea of losing either Keith or Glen was just too unfathomable to contemplate – to lose both, excruciating and more than my mind and body could bear. As I sat waiting, I turned my thoughts to happier times, to little things I loved about them both - to how I'd met Glen and to our life together:

I met Glen in my junior year in high school, when besides selling advertising, writing feature stories, and being an assistant editor, I helped a couple of 'hunt and peck' sports writers type up their finished copy. One of those was Glen Snodgrass, who seemed to me at the time to be something of an enigma. I remember thinking: He's obviously intelligent, a good writer, and articulate. Strange - he claims school is a waste of time.

I'm always astounded by the subtlety of his mind and his incredible ability to triangulate – to know a bit of this and a bit of that and, best of all, to make connections and draw conclusions from it all – like no one else I've ever known.

It is Glen who is first to recognize when one of the kids acts out in some way that indicates they need some alone time with one of us. He is sensitive to their needs and to mine, often organizing a spur of the moment way to meet that need. It might be something as simple as a trip to the dump or Davis Lumber and Hardware for a plumbing part or garden supplies; or it could be as involved as a day hike to the top of Mt. Tamalpais. It doesn't matter – it's a special time for a dad-kid chat.

He was a member of the debate team back in high school - excellent training, so talking is something he does well. I love that rich resonant voice of his and the way he enunciates his words with a casual precision. I can already tell that Mark will take after him.

Glen lifts my mind and my heart. I laugh when in the middle of a discussion I at last realize he's playing Devil's Advocate, taking the opposite argument from what I know he believes, just for the sake of a lively philosophical or political wrangle with the kids or with friends. Even though I'm wise to him and his foolery, he sometimes catches me off guard, deliberately taking a stance contrary to mine just to see what kind of a rise he can get out of me.

He does a million little thoughtful things for me, too. Like last month when he secretly bundled all the items in the bottom of our gigantic wicker ironing basket – those clothing items I always "postpone", sometimes for so long that the kids have outgrown them by the time I surrender and iron them. Anyway, he took them to Lorraine, the Ironing Lady, and a week later brought them back all freshly ironed. What a nice surprise!

Interestingly, when he has done a load of laundry, vacuumed the carpet, or helped with some household chore, he has never resented it or viewed it as "helping" me. In spite of that, I have always thought of it as such, feeling somehow inadequate for not being able to do what I consider my job by myself. Intellectually, I know that I have done my part, as I've worked part- or full-time nearly all of our married life; emotionally, there is still that pervasive self-deprecating notion that I've somehow failed, when I can't maintain the house and the kids perfectly by myself. Glen, who helped his mother with household chores and financially ever since his father died when he was eleven, did his best to negate what he perceived as a silly idea: "It's my house, too - and these are my kids."

We balance each other. Even as high school juniors way back in 1948, we recognized that unique simpatico. The day we first met back in the News Shack at Tacoma's Lincoln High School, we became good friends, finding each other intellectual equals with similar interests. We almost immediately started spending time together in and outside of school. We've been together, at least in spirit, ever since.

I've heard it said that even atheists pray in foxholes. This was my foxhole: "I haven't prayed much for a long time, but God, if you're listening, I hope you'll do something to help us.

My Prayers Went Unanswered

My memory remains fuzzy about just how our new living arrangements were made, but I learned that the Unitarian Ladies group provided much of the labor of moving us into a temporary home, a three-bedroom apartment on the north side of town, not far from the high school. My mother and stepfather arrived from Southern California; Glen's family from Seattle flew in, as well. Together we waited and prayed.

My prayers went unanswered.

Keith never regained consciousness and died on January 4, 1971. The Rev. Bob Senghas from the Unitarian Church of Davis, where we had been members since our arrival in that town, came to the apartment into which we had been moved immediately after he heard of Keith's death. After extending his condolences, he asked the hard question, "Do you have plans for Keith's burial."

"Glen and I once talked about death and dying. Because we have moved so often, we don't have a solid sense of belonging to any certain place. The one time I visited my father's grave in Tacoma, we agreed that we didn't like the 'final resting place' concept for us or for our children. We said that when the time came, we didn't want our children to be haunted by the idea they had to visit and care for our graves in perpetuity."

"So are you thinking of cremation?" he asked.

"Yes, I think that's best. In the abstract, we have preferred the idea of cremation." So I made this first decision. Bob helped me make arrangements for Keith's cremation and for his ashes to be scattered at sea.

After that, in preparation for the memorial service, the children and I spent what seemed like hours reminiscing with Bob about some of Keith's antics as a young child. "Remember the time in Albany, when we searched high and low for our missing turtle?" Laurie reminded us.

"Oh, yes, he must have been close to three then 'cause Mark was in Kindergarten, I think."

Anyway, he kept following us around, saying "Mom, it's on the garage roof!" We all kept shushing him and saying, "No, Keith, the turtle can't get up on the garage roof!"

"I remember feeling more than a little chagrined that we had ignored him when, as I was peeling potatoes at the kitchen sink, I glanced out the window and noticed my yellow pot holder mitt on the roof of the detached garage. And then it was so funny to hear that smug little voice, saying, 'I told you, Mommy,' as I retrieved the mitt with a long-handled rake and found the little turtle safely ensconced within."

"And then there was the time …I think it may have been our friend Jan Cross who called and jokingly told us, 'Keith was so cute! He came to our door like the Avon Lady with a box full of treasures, saying, 'I'm earning some money for a birthday present for my mom.'"

"I remember her saying that the treasures he offered included some old pieces of rope, balls of rubber bands, and several pre-loved Golden Books. What powers of persuasion! She went on to say that she had made a purchase, intrigued by his unusual awareness of the needs and feelings of others," I said.

"What I remember most about Keith," Rev. Senghas added, "is that whatever he did, he did with his own unique style and enthusiasm. He loved to talk – and he always seemed to know what he was talking about. He was high-spirited and adventuresome like any healthy boy his age."

"Talk! Oh, my! From the time he learned to talk, I'd yearn for his naptime. He'd say, 'But, Mom, I'm not tired,' to which I'd reply, 'That very well may be, Keith, but my ears are tired. They need a rest.' As a little guy, he always giggled at that – 'ears tired!' Little did he know.

Only 12 years old, but he seemed already to be developing such a sense of self. He received a birthday check from his grandparents for his December birthday. The first thing he bought was a poster for his room. As he read its words, he said, "These words describe me, Mom. 'If a man does not keep pace with his companions, perhaps it is because he hears a different drummer.'"

Plagued by attention deficit disorder (ADD), as well as a learning disability in his early years, he had the misfortune of following in the footsteps of four older siblings who excelled in school. However, by sixth grade Keith settled down and became a much better student, thanks to Robert E. Willett, a teacher at West Davis Intermediate School, who took a special interest in him and discovered his best learning style. Even so, he still claimed that Thoreau had written those lines just for him.

I won't mention any names here, but that fourth grade teacher who hadn't enjoyed teaching young boys almost ruined school for Keith. She made up her mind that Keith wasn't going to learn anyway, so when there weren't enough copies of reading and math materials to go around her too-large class, she sent him home with illegible faded dittoes. When he couldn't read them, his homework suffered. She said that she thought he might be dyslexic or retarded. We claimed that anyone holding a five-minute conversation with Keith could tell he was highly intelligent. We asked that he be tested. When the test results came back, he immediately received better grades and better treatment. A clear case of *dysteachia*!

In keeping with the thoughts and feelings of the poster, the kids suggested, "Let's play the music he liked for the memorial service – not churchy music. He loved Simon and Garfunkle and the Beatles." We chose some of his favorites: Bridge over Troubled Waters, Hey, Jude, and El Condor Pasa." Everyone agreed without a second's concern about whether people might think these choices inappropriate.

"What about flowers?" Bob asked?"

"I don't think I want a lot of flowers delivered to the church. Let's ask people to make a donation to the Burn Center if they wish to do something."

"I think we should just have two red roses," Marci suggested.

With tears suddenly flooding my eyes, "Oh, that's a great idea. When he was about ten he had an appendectomy. As we were leaving from a visit to his hospital room, we asked if we could bring him anything. I'll never forget that 'Poor Pitiful Pearl' voice of his, 'Some red roses, maybe?' I remember that we took him some with baby's breath."

Imagine, a ten year old boy asking for roses!

After Glen's regaining consciousness long enough for me to express my love and what I now know was my final good-bye, I got word just hours before Keith's memorial service that Glen, too, had died.

How will we get through this day?

That night, Keith's school and scout chums and their parents, friends and neighbors, friends of our teenagers and their parents, church members, as well as family who came from Southern California, Oregon and Washington, and, of course, Glen's

19

colleagues, crowded the Unitarian Church of Davis. I've never felt so cold - an unrelenting chill.

Even in tragedy I sought approval. All my life, I accepted someone else's expectations and values as my own, without much exploration or evaluation. My only role models, for behavior at a memorial service for my own loved ones, were Jacqueline Kennedy and Coretta Scott King, so, like them, I maintained my composure. I smiled bravely and thanked everyone for coming.

I quietly fell apart inside, hiding my real feelings, thinking: If I can just get through this night. This is the nightmare no one dreams could/would ever befall them, and it is happening to us. It is inconceivable! Why can't I remember the name of this woman who is trying to console me? I know her, but I can't even place how I know her.

A second memorial service was held two nights later. I'm sorry to say that I remember very little of Glen's memorial service or of seeing the people in attendance. It was only through looking at the Guest Book later that I came to realize that attendees included colleagues and friends from New Orleans, the San Francisco Bay Area, as well as faculty and staff from the University and President's Office in Berkeley. Family from out of town had stayed on after Keith's service, knowing by that time that Glen, too, had died.

The family hovered and seemed expansively sympathetic. I really just wanted to climb into bed, pull the blankets up over my head and drown out the sympathetic voices in the other room.

Truth be told, I'd just like everyone to go home. I know they are trying to help. But it is only making things worse. The only people I really want around me right now are my children and their friends. Sharing memories, laughing and crying together are somehow a comfort. Why do I feel self-conscious about our laughing? All those solemn faces surrounding us, looking on so sympathetically make our laughter seem somehow vulgar and inappropriate. But we need that release and relief. Through remembering the good times, we can relieve the excruciating pain of the present – if only for a few short minutes.

I guess that at some level I knew the family and our friends needed to deal with their grief in their own way by helping the kids and me get through this. Relatives took the kids shopping for shoes and new clothes; my mother took Laurie to a beauty shop to have her singed hair trimmed.

Carolyn Benner, a close friend and someone for whom the three girls babysat all the years we'd been in Davis, earlier became the communications center, fielding calls and sharing medical information. Shipley Walters, another friend who had been a neighbor from when we lived in Metairie, Louisiana, but who now also lived in Davis, kept the list of contributions of food, money and labor. Friends and acquaintances spent hours cleaning furniture, laundering and dry-cleaning our smoke-permeated clothing, supplying bedding, and restoring those of our belongings that could be salvaged. As the grimness of our situation became known, a steady stream of casseroles and desserts were delivered to our door - enough to feed the army of relatives and friends, who arrived from far and near.

I recently found, tucked in the back of the Leaves of Memory guest book, a browned and tattered list of over one hundred people who made contributions of furnishings for our new apartment – everything from linens to labor for laundry and dry cleaning. Keith's Boy Scout troop held a bottle drive for the memorial fund that was set up for the Burn Center; a group of high school kids formed a work party at a warehouse. At the time, I was oblivious to all the activity to support us that occurred during the two to three weeks after the fire. Grateful, but benumbed, probably best describes my condition at the time.

We somehow survived those difficult days. Afterward, I wrote a thank-you brochure to those who sent cards and letters, or attended the memorial service:

> So many people have expressed the desire to 'do something for the family.' We want you all to know how much you are doing – the comfort we all gained – and are gaining – from your words, your thoughts, and your presence.
>
> Our every physical need has been met so admirably – and unbelievably. The doctors and nurses – mostly friends – made a heroic, round-the-clock effort to save Glen and Keith. We know they could not have received better or more loving care anywhere.
>
> Further, we have had so much love in our family – and continue to have – so much joy – so many happy, happy memories. We are so lucky – we have no regrets. We understood one another, accepted each other – weaknesses, faults and all.

We loved and we learned from one another how to face life and what it may bring.

We are enclosing the eulogies from the Memorial Services in the hope that you may gain some comfort – and hope – from the knowledge that their lives touched many, and in deep appreciation for your love, your thoughtfulness – for your strength, which somehow must have transfused us.

We would like to share with you a quote we received. It expresses our feelings so well:

"We are only permitted to grieve because we have been privileged to love – and to escape grief is too great a price to pay."

The Snodgrass Family
January 7, 1971

The Unthinkable

People who think dying is the worst thing don't know a thing about life.
-Sue Monk Kidd in *The Secret Life of Bees*

When the unthinkable hits the 6 o'clock news, you can turn it off. When it happened to me it was as though my whole life had been ripped apart. The death of my son - my youngest – and in a home fire? It was beyond belief! And the person I loved most in all the world, the person to whom I had always turned, in good times and bad, was also gone.

The wrong one of us died. Glen was the competent one. He could have managed all of this - so much better.

Glen clearly had a great future; it was already apparent that bigger and better things were in store for him. The medical school was in good shape now; the ten-year forecast for University-wide health science needs that he prepared for the President's Office was finished and on its way to the Legislature. He celebrated when the UC Davis faculty overwhelmingly voted its approval. He reveled in getting things started and fine-tuned to run smoothly and then moving on to the next challenge. We never knew when that time to move on would come, but Glen always said that if an administrator is doing his job, he is not indispensable.

I just hope to heavens that this family is fine-tuned enough to run smoothly in his absence. How will I manage? He was more than indispensable to us - to me. He was far more than an administrator here.

Try as I might to show a brave front, I sat staring off into space, oblivious to all that was going on around me. I took long solitary walks in the dark hours of the pre-dawn morning, trying to come to grips with what happened to us, preferring my own company to that of sympathizers who offered heartfelt yet what to me seemed meaningless trite phrases. Anger surfaced again and again. I kept waking night after night praying that this was a nightmare, hoping against hope to reach over and find Glen there in bed beside me. If only…

I have four surviving children. I have to be there for them. They can't lose a mother; they've already lost a father and a brother. But in many ways, they have lost a mother, too - at least, as they have always known her.

For weeks, if not months, I felt powerless, unloved, and wounded - a gaping hole in my heart. I was almost afraid to go to sleep for fear I'd dream a recurring convoluted dream of being told that Keith had not really died, but instead had been secretly taken to a Texas Burn Center, where they were successfully treating his catastrophic burns. In this dream they said, "We told you he had died, because we were sure he would die. We thought we'd save you the pain and suffering of going through it again." I wept tears of joy when in the dream they told me, "Now he's doing quite well. It looks as though he'll recover and need to be brought home for skin grafting and rehabilitation." And then, when I awoke I shed tears of desolation.

Due to my wish to regain my memories of Glen and Keith as they were before the fire, I decided not to view their bodies, nor did I give that option to the children. In retrospect, I can see that there may be good reasons for viewing the body of a loved one. I now wonder if seeing his body after he died might have precluded my disturbing dreams and my guilty delusion that he was still alive somewhere. Through no fault of my own, in my invention, poor little Keith had gone through all of that suffering in rehabilitation way off in a strange hospital without the comfort of having his mother by his side. How alone and abandoned he must have felt, I thought. Even in the early waking hours after such a vision, I wondered whether, in fact, doctors deceived and betrayed me; I felt confused, guilty, remorseful, and yet thrilled that my young son was still alive - until I came fully awake.

Are my dreams a way for my subconscious to keep Glen and Keith with me a while longer? I can't tell anyone. I am ashamed and a little frightened, too. I already have a memory problem. Not this, too. Is this another symptom of an unbalanced mind?

I dreamed some form of this same dream over and over again until I finally broached the subject with Dr. Benner. He assured me that Keith had, indeed, died. He also told me that these kinds of recurring dreams are normal and natural. Sometimes a way of helping the bereaved keep the person they've lost near them a little longer. Once I talked about the dream with him, it never recurred.

I turned to friends, to church and to family to help me feel better. When they couldn't, they felt defeated and deflated -- and I felt more and more isolated, more than I ever could have imagined possible. People kept consoling and assuring me with phrases, such as:

"You're young, Joan; you'll marry again."
"You have four wonderful children."
"Time will heal!"

That does not console me! I don't think they understand.

I often felt betrayed by women acquaintances. Rather than meet me face to face, some would cross to the other side of the supermarket or street if they caught sight of me. A part of me understood; it was probably because they didn't know what to say. Another part felt shunned. I'd come home after such a non-encounter and phone them, saying, "I saw you at State Market this afternoon, but you got away from me before I had a chance to say Hello." And then I'd take part in a bit of small talk to help her feel more comfortable, so that perhaps she would speak to me the next time we ran into each other.

Some loyal and caring friends invited me for coffee or lunch. When they occasionally invited me for dinner, however, the husband would vanish into his study the minute the meal was over, leaving me feeling I was not fit company for couples. Later, as I learned more about bereavement, I came to realize that his own unresolved grief over losing Glen, in the prime of his life, undoubtedly left this colleague ill-equipped to carry on a conversation with me. Some of these husbands had even been on the medical team that took care of Glen and Keith. Understandably, their sense of loss may have involved double jeopardy – loss on more than one level: a sense of failure for not having been able to save the life of a patient, but also that of a colleague and friend.

An occasional more open man would confess that Glen's death and visiting with me provided a painful reminder of his own mortality. Some said, "All I can think of when I see you are those poor kids and how painful this must be for you, Joni."

And when I see you, all I can think of are all the plans Glen and I had for our future – a future we'll never have together.

I gradually separated from many of our married couple friends, relationships that had developed mostly through Glen's medical school and university professional affiliations. I tended to feel like a fifth wheel, the lone back seat passenger in what I continued to perceive as a couple world. This isolation, of course, turned my thoughts to doubting my value, except as a part of the couple we had been.

**Best friends Lila Field and Bill Sandman witness
our wedding vows on January 25, 1951**

Life Goes On, However Lamely

In three words, I can sum up everything I know about life: It goes on.
- Robert Frost

The relatives went back to their respective lives, checking in from time to time to see how the kids and I were doing.

Shipley Walters, my next-door neighbor and rock-solid friend from when we lived in New Orleans, had moved to Davis when Glen recruited her husband, Dick, to head up the computer program for the new medical school. They were with me every step of the way after the fire. Shipley called me daily to ask of my plans for the day. Even when I felt saddest, loneliest, and most wanted to be isolated, she ignored my predisposition and cheered me on, letting me know that she was thinking about me and was there for me whether I wanted her or not. Shipley gave me vital support during those days, weeks and months – support I didn't even know I needed.

My world is confusing and sad. I resent her calls; they interrupt my wallowing in self-pity. Of course, that's what she intends. I suppose it is what I need.

By this time, they (the omnipresent "they" who made things just magically happen in those early days) had moved some of my own furniture into the three-bedroom apartment in North Davis, making it feel marginally more like home than the hand-me-downs we had at first had.

How grateful I am to have my own bed, the one I shared with Glen for so many years. Somehow it comforts me to lie on his side of the bed, even though I know, intellectually, that this is a new mattress, new pillow, on which he never slept. Never mind. I let my imagination give me whatever solemn solace it can find.

The three girls temporarily shared the master bedroom of the apartment until Valerie returned to college; Mark bunked by himself in another, and I slept in the third. Crowded but temporary, I assured everyone.

"What day do you want to go back to Portland, Val? We'd better make your plane reservations."

Notice, I asked "when," not "Do you want to go back to college" to finish up the current semester. Maintain. Smile bravely. Hard as it may be, life does have to go on. Their dad would have wanted them to go on with their lives. Of course, she'll go back to school in time for her mid-year finals.

What was I thinking? I must have been deranged.

Neither of us realized how difficult it would be to not have the day-to-day solidarity of the family during this time of recovery. Letters frequently contained snippets of her misery:

"I feel so alone, Mom."

"It's hard to concentrate. I've read this same chapter over three times and I still don't know what it says."

And plaintively, "How is everyone doing in Davis? How are you?" Not even telephone calls reassured either one of us.

Glen's aunt and uncle, George and Eva Faulkner, lived in Portland not far from Reed College, where Val was a sophomore. They provided a place for her to go on weekends to get away - a place, yes, but more importantly people who had some inkling of what she was going through. Eva taught her to crochet. George, often thought of as rather taciturn, engaged her in philosophical discussions, and always had a story to tell about a recent fishing trip. Valerie recalls that her cousin, Kirby, who had recently moved to Portland, sometimes joined them for a home-cooked meal or a game of bridge. Eva would make her special popcorn, seasoned with bacon grease that she strained and kept refrigerated just for those occasions – "incredibly delicious! – if not healthy," Valerie recalls. They happily offered her a place to go for comfort, familiar conversation, and she is quick to add, "the bane of all college students – a comfortable place to do my laundry."

Asking, "How did you do on your finals?" would be a fruitless question, as professors at Reed don't post or discuss grades unless they are unsatisfactory. Believing that comparisons among students undermine the spirit of a cooperative intellectual community, they typically return papers and projects with comments rather than grades. No news was good news.

Marci and Laurie were Varsity and JV cheerleaders at the time of the fire. An immediate question came up about the home basketball game the Friday following the memorial services. "Do you want to go?" I asked.

"Yes, I suppose we should. It's our responsibility." They donned their freshly cleaned uniforms and with bright forced smiles joined their squad members in leading cheers.

It must be torture to get out there in front of these crowds and act as though nothing has happened.

A few weeks later both girls were elected to the Homecoming Court. "Do you suppose they voted for us out of pity?" they wondered aloud.

"Did you wonder last spring when the student body elected you? They weren't voting for you out of compassion then, were they?" I asked.

No, of course not. Their questioning at this time gives evidence that a tragedy such as this can quickly deflate the fragile self-confidence of adolescents.

I borrowed a sewing machine, bought some material, and made a dress for each of the girls, followed by the dreaded shoe shopping. "What? You mean I can't wear clogs?" I can only imagine the thoughts that must have been going through their minds as they walked out onto the gym floor. I know I could feel the sympathetic eyes, real or imagined, as I walked into the gym with Mark and my friends, trying my best to be invisible.

Laurie's escort, class president Josh Stein, sported not only a carnation in his lapel, but a large curly Afro in his Caucasian hair. While they sat in the stands, Josh unearthed a pizza from beneath a denim jacket he wore under his blazer. He offered to go fifty-fifty with Laurie. She declined.

I wish that Glen could be here to share this moment with Marci and Laurie. He has always been so proud of his family. He will miss all of their special days – graduation, weddings, and babies. Life isn't fair. It just is!

I fast-forwarded to all of the other important days in their lives that he would miss. Life goes on - however lamely. Valerie persevered back at college - alone and isolated even with regular phone calls and letters. Marci enjoyed the company of a very tight group of friends who practically lived at our house, but Laurie and Mark, especially vulnerable at fifteen and thirteen, felt detached. Dr. Donald Langley, Chief of Psychiatry at the medical school, as well as a friend, talked with them once or twice right after the fire, but they seemed reserved – perhaps it was too soon, maybe they felt too guarded, defenseless, or exposed.

In fact, later they may have had the same insatiable need to pour out their grief that I had, but to whom could they go? Could they dare to open themselves to the pain? Had I known then what I know now, I would have been aware that the teen years under normal conditions have so much angst going on that the additional burden of grieving for one's father and little brother is too much to add. Grief work? At that age, it is much easier to tune out; turn off. Later, maybe, when they are not quite so vulnerable.

Laurie, eighteen months younger than Marci, remained on the fringes of Marci's group. She formed close friendships with high school junior Dave Scott, who lived three doors away, and classmate Allison Radford. They provided a welcome diversion, if not the deep emotional support, she needed at that time.

Being a friend means continuing to invite your friend to join in activities or to just give her a hug. Being a friend means not avoiding, but instead walking up to let her know that you're there for her, that you know what a difficult time this must be. This is hard for an adult to manage, but surely much more challenging for children or teens, just as the grieving process is much more difficult for them than for adults.

Cal Crabill, Laurie's math teacher, was the only one of her teachers who ever talked with her about the fire and the loss of her father and little brother. He checked in with her frequently to see how she was getting along, and to ask about Val, with whom he had had a special relationship, having been her math teacher throughout her three years at DHS. Years later at a high school reunion, several friends apologized to Laurie for not being there for her, saying they just did not know what to say, so they had said nothing.

After the excitement of answering questions for the fire department was over, Mark retreated to his room to bury himself in reading. Much later, he told me, "Mom, I felt like an outsider in my own home. All those girls."

I remember thinking that I was giving him space for teenage independence. How could I have known he felt isolated from what appeared to him a coterie of women? Had I known then what I know now, I would have had him and Laurie meeting with a therapist on a regular basis. What they needed was a "life coach" to help them do the grief work their sensitive instincts told them to avoid.

Life goes on, however feebly: insurance claims, retirement benefits, legal matters, and a partially destroyed house to be rebuilt. I found locating the records and papers required for all the bureaucratic demands frustrating, especially with my befuddled mind. Some days it seemed overwhelming. [For suggestions on organizing affairs for survivors, see Appendix III.)

We can live in this apartment for awhile, but I need to make a real home for us, a place where we can be comfortable, where the kids can invite their friends. I don't want to go back to the house on Mulberry Lane. I'm sure I would always smell that pungent smoke, even if only in my imagination.

I decided that the two garage-conversion rooms should be restored to their original usage – never again to present the possibility of a fire to trap a sleeping child – not there, not in that house. And three bedrooms would not be big enough for our family. In fact, there still weren't many houses available in Davis big enough for our family - even at its reduced size.

Jim Quick, the father of Laurie's friend, Ross, and our backyard over-the-fence neighbor, volunteered to be the general contractor for the rebuild of the Mulberry house. I'm eternally grateful to him for that and to the University Medical School staff for their help in wading through the mountains of paperwork involved with settling insurance, Social Security and the various applications that needed to be filled out for retirement benefits for me and the children.

It was several weeks before my emotions allowed me to put together a list of our losses for our insurance coverage. Even then, this proved to be a difficult task, as my memory played tricks on me. What was in that room? In what year had we purchased the TV? In the meantime, Jim Hilliard of State Farm Insurance took care of boarding up the house, inspections, estimates, and having our furniture cleaned, as well as our baby grand piano rebuilt and refinished.

Wise are the people who go through their homes with a digital camera, recording their belongings, room by room, adding to it as they acquire new belongings. This record, along with a list of items and their original purchase prices should be stored in a safety deposit box away from the property.

Housing was still at a premium in Davis, so I asked my advisors and the kids, "What do you think about our having a house built for us?" After not much discussion, I decided to build if we could find an appropriate lot. Verne Scott, the father of one of Marci's closest friends, persuaded Pat and Bill Williams, the owners of one of the two remaining lots on Elmwood Drive, an ideal location not far from where we had previously lived, to sell to us. Several friends, who lived within shouting distance on that street, including the Scott's and the Walter's, would be my stalwart support for many months – indeed, years.

Sam Harrison and Julian Youmans, two friends involved with real estate and development, gave me financial advice and introduced me to a reputable and creative builder, John Whitcombe. The process began. I spent hours perusing architectural magazines for ideas and working with Whitcombe's architect after I drew up preliminary sketches. While this served as something of a distraction, it did not lessen the deep depression I felt.

The design of this home would not only meet our family's needs, it would satisfy my paranoia about fire. We designed each room in the house (except for two of the three bathrooms) with an easy exit to the outdoors. A redwood-faced balcony across the back of the house with stairs led down to the swimming pool/deck area. Mark's room would have a sliding door to his own private balcony. Sliding glass doors from the dining room, living room and every bedroom led to either the side or back yard. Aside from all the easy escape routes, the house would have all of the amenities of a normal house.

It was only much later when Marci and her husband Peter, who eventually bought the family home, remodeled the front of the house to be much more open that I realized how closed off I wanted to be when I designed the house. I didn't want to be seen. I still like privacy, and appreciate the fact that our new house has no windows visible from the street.

In the meantime, life became even more complicated in the small apartment in which we would live until the new house became more than a blueprint drawing.

The Infirmary

A trip to the orthodontist added yet another stress factor. After X-rays, Dr. Horrigan greeted me with, "Laurie and Marci's wisdom teeth should be removed, Joan. If we don't do it right away, there is risk of undermining all of the orthodontia that we've done up to now." I made an arrangement with the oral surgeon for impacted wisdom teeth extraction for both girls early in the summer.

We have a real investment in those Pepsodent smiles. Glen and I laughingly said that we'd personally paid for the Horrigan swimming pool, so ignoring this warning doesn't seem like a good option.

Valerie came home from college at Spring Break, again complaining of a lot of back pain. She had been diagnosed with scoliosis as an eighth grader, and had worn a Milwaukee back brace for two years before having a spinal fusion as a sophomore in high school. Now her orthopedic surgeon and X-rays affirmed, "Her previous surgery was only partially successful. Her orthopedist told us that she needed another fusion to relieve the pain, but he didn't think this one would require casting or as much bed rest afterward."

Well, that was a relief for both Val and me, as the last spinal fusion resulted in three months in a full body cast in a hospital bed and six months with a walking cast. This had been quite a blow to a dedicated high school sophomore, whose life revolved around school.

I have no recollection of how it came about, but for the long recuperation after that first surgery, Pacific Bell installed at no charge to us an intercom system between each of her classrooms and her bedroom at home. This phone hook-up allowed her to continue to be a part of her classes.

Cal Crabill, her math teacher – the one teacher who had been supportive of Laurie after the fire – and Marge Kendall, her history teacher, visited Val weekly, bringing her handouts, homework and words of encouragement.

Her dad and friend Dick Walters occasionally lifted her onto a used wicker wheelchair we had found at a medical supply house – one that allowed her to lie flat while being transported out to the patio or into the family room. They sometimes loaded her into the back of the station wagon and took her to a drive-in movie. She could view the movie, read, watch TV or play ping-pong with the aid of prism glasses.

I've learned something from each of my children, but probably the most from Valerie, who at age six was diagnosed with Ehlers-Danlos syndrome, a collagen disease. From her example, as she suffered through round after round of sutures for moon-shaped lacerations from little falls that for another child might have resulted in only minor scrapes, I learned endurance, patience, and grace.

Glen and I managed her care at home after the last surgery – together. I'm grateful this surgery won't be as complicated. I should say, 'We're grateful!' After all, it is Valerie who will have to endure the pain and spend her whole summer convalescing. No doubt without a complaint – she is such a trooper!

My plate was getting pretty full. My mother, who lived in Southern California with my stepfather, came to the rescue. She rented an apartment nearby, so that she could help me run the "infirmary" during the summer months.

I welcomed her company, her support, and some of her home cooking. By this time, the kids were getting rather tired of the creamed tuna on toast, macaroni and cheese, and spaghetti meals that I had often prepared quickly when Glen was away on a trip or had a late dinner meeting. I wasn't hungry these days, and my psyche was treating mealtime as if Glen were just away – barely adequate, quick and easy, what you might call 'catch-as-catch-can'! Mom's home style cooking provided a welcome respite. The girls recovering from wisdom tooth extraction especially appreciated the delicious soups she delivered daily from her apartment kitchen.

It was about this time that I decided to try one of the new portable microwaves. Perhaps I would want one built-in at the new house. I bought one "on approval" from Sears and brought it home. The first night I baked potatoes – for six! Well, of course, I could have baked them in the oven in the same amount of time, and, further more, they would have tasted good! I returned the oven and did not plan to install one in the new house. (Eventually, of course, I did get another portable one for re-heating and defrosting.)

♠

Rebuilding and selling the Mulberry House was underway. Oral surgery for Laurie and Marci and orthopedic surgery for Valerie took place early in the summer. We hoped to move into the new house by the time school started in September.

I had ambivalent feelings about this new home. I felt more than a little guilty that I was to enjoy this comfort at the expense of Glen and Keith. Yet in another way it felt like restitution or redress of a terrible wrong that had been done to us. Perhaps the swimming pool and whatever luxuries I could give the children would alleviate, in some small way, their pain.

A paradox. Second thoughts, confusion, equivocation, and guilt – all rolled into one: ambivalence.

Eventually, Glen and Keith and happier times became visitors to my dreams. I would wake reliving some happy time; disappointment upon coming fully awake and aware would bring tears to my eyes. Grief experts write that you have to go through a period of feeling sad, defeated, sorry for yourself, wondering interminably, "Why us?" I anxiously awaited the arrival of that third stage they talk about - that feeling better state; it seemed slow in coming.

A brown corduroy beanbag chair made for me by a group of Marci's friends for my birthday was a constant source of comfort.

Pity parties remain a common occurrence as I curl up in an almost fetal position in that chair for many an hour, staring into the fire in the fireplace, reminding myself that times will get better.

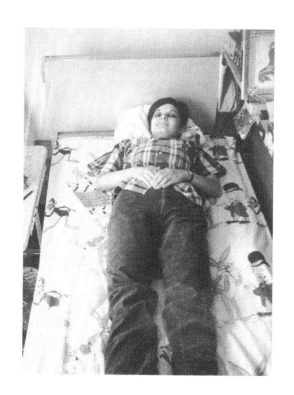

Anger is an Acid

"Anger is an acid that can do more harm to the vessel in which it stands than to anything on which it is poured." - Unknown

As the numbness wore off and the depression deepened, little bits of anger began to creep in. Why us? The fire investigation proved that the gas wall furnace between Keith and Mark's bedroom had caused the fire. I had noticed the smell of gas a couple of weeks before Christmas '70 and called P.G. &E. They came to the house, tested it and proclaimed, "No real problem! I tightened a nut, but there's nothing wrong with this furnace." Evidence later showed, however, that a high wind caused a flare-up at a leaky valve and ignited the cedar-paneled wall with its highly flammable finish.

I fume retroactively at the cavalier attitude the PG & E repairman had shown about a gas leak that eventually led to the death of my husband and youngest son. And why had the previous owners put that highly flammable paneling in that room anyway?

I knew it was irrational, but it nettled me that Mark spent so much time at the burn site. He seemed to relish all the excitement of the fire department's investigation and the attention he was getting with their endless questions. As I learned more about grief in adolescents, I came to realize that this distraction is one way for children to ignore the panic and deny the grief that lies dormant just below the surface. Several people told him, "You're the man of the family now, Mark. You've got to be brave and help your mom." So I suppose taking over during the investigation helped him to feel he was assuming that responsibility.

But he is just a boy!

My anger and irritation aren't well focused. I can hardly be angry with Keith or Glen. Who or what will be the next target?

♠

About this time, I noticed a duplication of charges on Glen's most recent American Express Card bill for his motel and restaurant expenses during his Berkeley stay. Almost a dozen of the items were listed – and then listed again. It appeared that a key-punch operator had inadvertently duplicated these items, thus doubling the bill. "Please send me the signed invoices for all of the charges on this statement. It looks as though there's a keyboard error."

I heard nothing back from them until next statement time, when I received an overdue notice and a penalty charge for the half of the bill I had not paid. I again asked for the invoices, and indicated I was unwilling to pay the bill until they gave me proof of charges. The next month they started phoning me; they ignored my explanations and requests, with what ultimately became tantamount to harassment - another target for my anger. It took a call from my attorney to get this matter cleared up.

Building a new home presented even more opportunities for distraction and despair. One day I arrived at the front entry in time to see the newly constructed rough-hewn wooden stairway to the second floor of the new house. "These are just temporary stairs, aren't they?" I asked.

"No, these are the stairs," the developer replied.

"Johnny, these are horrible! We designed an entry hall the size of a room, but still the front door bangs against the back of these ugly stairs?" A custom-built gracious spiral stair of black wrought iron with a curved wooden railing and carpet-covered steps proved to be a solution, albeit expensive and causing yet another delay.

Next, when they delivered the kitchen cabinets – already later than planned – I could see obvious flaws that were accentuated by the dark finish. "Sorry about those dings in the wood, Joan. We can replace them, but it'll mean another month's delay in getting you into the house," the contractor said. I really wanted to get us settled into our new home before the kids started school in the fall, so I compromised and agreed when told they could be sanded and painted so that the dents would not be noticed. Not what I wanted, but oh, well. New stress and yet another focus for anger.

That wrath would last a long time, as I weekly, if not daily, washed the fingerprints off those white cupboards, which had to be painted and repainted over the next twenty years.

There were endless financial decisions to be made, as well as many of long-lasting consequence in terms of decorating the new house. Paint or wallpaper in the dining room, bedrooms and baths? Color of flooring and counter materials in the bathrooms and kitchen? What kind of carpet for the floors and what color?

Endless details surfaced that often seemed frivolous and superfluous; things such as choosing doorknobs, drapery trims, and placement of electric outlets. Delberta Hurley, an interior designer friend, and I became inseparable as we scoured the market place for perfect pieces of furniture and accessories for the new home.

Delberta is more interested in these details than I. Who cares in the grand scheme of things? Well, it may make a difference to me later, perhaps. I'll do as she says.

Geremia Pools installed a large rectangular coke-bottle green pool in the back yard complete with diving board and all the electrical accoutrements. Verne and Dave Scott and friends installed a fence around the perimeter of the yard. The final touch was a removable water polo backboard at one end of the pool, where Dave and Mark practiced.

Dave later went on to become a six-time Ironman Champion and the first inductee into the Ironman Hall of Fame. All those laps in our pool may even have contributed to his success. I can still hear in my mind's ear Dave's flip turns as he swam laps every night.

The house was finally painted, wall papered, and carpeted. The draperies were hung, and we moved into an almost completed home. For months a few final finishing touches remained undone, but seemed low on the contractor's priority list.

The final motivation for him came several months later, however, when Yolo Family Service Agency asked me if they could show our home at their annual fundraising home tour. I agreed, partially because I knew this would get all of the detailing of the house completed – pronto! I half-jokingly told the contractor, "I think I'll post little signs above every missing wall plug "This house was built by John Whitcombe." It worked! His crew arrived the very next week to start on the inventory of things he'd put off for months. Small victory!

Not Ready for Houseguests

After a time, I remembered an old English saying my grandmother had told me when things went awry in my young life: "Joni, it's an ill wind, indeed, that blows no good!" I pondered endlessly, "What good will this ill wind bring?" I could find no answer.

Still depressed, I continued to feel angry – still angry with the law that prevented the ambulances from taking Glen and Keith directly to the Medical Center rather than to our inadequate little community hospital, deluding myself that it could have made a difference. I was angry with P.G.&E. for not catching a leaky valve that would have prevented the fire from ever happening. I wrote letters to the Governor, hoping to change the "nearest hospital" law. I brought suit on behalf of the family against P.G.&E., who offered a settlement the first day of the trial, immediately after the opening statement of our attorney.

Four nervous somber teenagers, sitting in the front row of the Courthouse, undoubtedly cast doubt on whether they, as defendants, have a chance of winning such a case. I don't care about a financial settlement; I just want P.G.&E to change their cavalier ways.

♠

We got through that summer vacillating between interior design and running a twenty-four hour a day infirmary. We got moved into the new house on schedule before school started with only a few small details left, including some planting, according to the landscape designer's plan. My father-in-law from Longview, Washington, asked if he might do that for us. He and Glen's mother arrived for an extended stay.

I always considered Glen's mother, Millie Snodgrass, all one could ever wish for in a mother-in-law. From the very first moment we met, she opened her heart and her home to me. Time after time during the first few years of our marriage, Mom, as I came to call her, came to our rescue. When our finances were so tenuous after Valerie was born and we decided to drop out of Reed and leave Portland, we moved in temporarily with her and Glen's younger brother, who was still in high school. Glen commuted to the University of Washington in Seattle in hopes of completing his undergraduate degree. I got a secretarial job with Tacoma attorneys, Mike Manza and James Moceri. Glen's mom took care of Valerie - and loved every minute of it.

Soon the round-trip commute from Tacoma to Seattle became too arduous. Glen found a part-time job, collecting delinquent bills for the business office at Swedish Hospital in Seattle. We soon moved into an apartment there and then into a two-bedroom unit in the less expensive High Point Housing Project, as it was subsidized, based on income. When Marci was born, it was Glen's mother who came to take care of Valerie while I was in the hospital. She stayed on to help me for a few days after I came home with the new baby.

It was some time after this that she, having been widowed since Glen was eleven, became reacquainted with and married a recently widowed old friend from high school days. Our relationship changed somewhat with her move from Tacoma to Longview, even though only a few hours away. It changed even further when Glen and I joined the First Unitarian Church in Seattle.

When our children had expressed an interest in attending Sunday school with their cousins, we tried their church for a time, but found the teachings clashed with our more secular humanistic convictions. We visited several different churches and soon became devoted fans of Rev. Peter Raible, whose sermons stimulated us and were in harmony with our belief system.

While Millie, a life-long Methodist, had always been active in her church, an important part of her life, she had never been judgmental about Glen's past disinterest in religion; she had always accepted his more liberal views and his own search for truth. Reford, a Southern Baptist, however, was appalled and disheartened by this new "unenlightened, heathen, and irreverent" involvement of ours. So much so, that upon hearing the news of our joining the First Unitarian Church, he immediately drove across the state, from Longview to Seattle, in an attempt to dissuade us from inflicting these teachings on our children. He said, "They, for sure, will never enter Heaven with this kind of religious upbringing. "

This was a conflict we never overcame. In order to complete the landscaping plan, Millie and Reford came to Davis shortly after we moved into the Elmwood house some nine months after the fire. I would have coped more easily had it been just Millie; but sadly, the difference between Reford's and my ideology created friction when time after time he sermonized to my children with his fundamental beliefs. Under normal circumstances, I might have been more tolerant, but this was not a time for someone to be speaking to my children about heaven, hell and their danger of not being 'saved.'

42

Sadly, we locked horns over this issue. Eventually, I gathered my courage and explained that we really needed more alone time, all but telling them to go home. They returned to Washington.

Knowing Glen's mom as I did, I think that she understood my dilemma, although we never again discussed it. It was clear even to me that I had a much shorter fuse than usual. I was intellectually grateful, but emotionally exposed. It was too early for houseguests and what seemed like twenty-four/seven of "being on" – playing a part and wearing a mask. At the time of Glen and Keith's deaths, and even at this time, my own grief was so overwhelming that I fear that I, thoughtlessly, was not sensitive to how great Millie's grief must still have been. She, too, had lost a child and a grandchild.

A Mexicana Diversion

Late in 1971, my brother Bill and his wife, Mickey, suggested (nay – insisted!) that I go with them on a trip they had planned to visit friends in Mexico City and Toluca. They thought this would be a good distraction for me, even though I'd never met their Mexican friends and spoke little to no Spanish.

They had met these people through their son, Val, when he was attending a military academy in Tacoma, Washington, where both Mexican families sent their sons for an intensified English language experience. Bill and Mickey often invited the boys to their home for weekends and holidays. In return, Val had gone several times to Mexico for holidays with their families.

With some reluctance I decided to go along.

Marguerita Ballesteros, and her driver, met us at the airport. Enriqué drove us "home" to a most opulent house in the Pedregal, an exclusive area of Mexico City. We entered the grounds through a locked gate with an intercom, along a circular driveway to large double doors. The entry hallway, about twelve feet wide and forty feet long, almost as wide as our living room at home and about twice as long, was decorated with antique chairs and settees, paintings, and lush verdant plantings.

As we entered, to the left was a small study and to the right a large living room with several conversation areas. A formal dining room, that would easily seat twenty-four, separated the living room and a large kitchen. In my several visits with the Ballesteros family, I ate in the formal dining room only once, and that was a large sit-down formal meal with guests. By this time, they considered us family – "Mi casa es su casa," the common Latina phrase, aptly applied to this visit and to my every subsequent one.

Midway down the hall, doors on the left led to an indoor, almost Olympic-sized, swimming pool, surrounded by tables, chairs, lounges, and luxurious tropical plantings. At the end of the hall, and to the right, was a family room and casual eating area. Under Senora's place at the table was a button, which she pressed with her toe to summon Alicia, a maid, who scurried in to provide whatever was needed from the kitchen, which was conveniently placed between the formal dining room and the family room.

The kitchen had a well-equipped large walk-in pantry. Stairs from the kitchen led to the laundry and living quarters of an older woman, Guillermo's nanny since his birth. Her only task these days was to launder and iron Guillermo's shirts, just as she had all of his life.

The cook, other maids, a gardener, and Enriqué all seemed to arrive early in the morning before anyone else was up and about. The gardener worked on the grounds five days a week, pruning, weeding, mowing, and planting. There never seemed to be a leaf out of place in their peaceful, always flowering garden.

Marguerita confessed that they didn't need all of this household help, but that it was their duty to provide employment for as many people as possible. They treated them well, providing houses for them and their families, as well as what was considered a generous salary and medical treatment, when necessary.

The bedroom wing, adjoining one wall of the swimming pool area, was separated at night from the rest of the house by a sliding steel door they locked into place when everyone was within. Each of the children's bedrooms looked very much like what we would consider a master bedroom suite, each with its own private bath and dressing area. Each bedroom had large windows covered by attractive sculptured metal bars that resembled mullions more than the burglar bars they were. Guillermo, whose engineering firm constructed the house, installed these special security measures in the design of the house, mindful of the fact that intruders had murdered two of their friends in their beds not long before he designed and built this home.

Marguerita, having been told of our fire before my arrival, sensed that I might be concerned about being locked in during the night. She explained to me how I could open the sliding bars in Laura and Ilena's room where I slept, should I need to get out. I immediately felt Maguis, as she was called and which distinguished her from her namesake eldest daughter, a kindred soul. I found her beautiful inside, as well as out. We became instant fast friends.

Maguis spent much time over the years in France where her father's family originated. Fluent in French, she longed to improve her English, too, as they often traveled to the United States. She told me that she practiced once a week with a nun, who became a friend. It was a blessing for me that she wished to work on her English, because my Spanish was "un poquito" and my French was not much better, even though I had studied French in high school and college.

The Rabelais in old French that Glen and I studied with Professor Woodbridge at Reed, all those years ago, did me little good in conversation with Maguis. In hindsight, living in California with its large Hispanic population as we now do, Spanish would have been a much better choice.

Guillermo, an engineer and major building contractor in Mexico, told me "My only problem is I have to work." As we visited the hotel that his engineering firm had just completed, Guillermo told us a story of the recent Grand Opening ceremony. As dignitaries exuded their praise to the architects and congratulated Guillermo and his company on this glorious addition to their city, they were interrupted by a leak. "We were struck with panic as some water came through the ceiling, as we knew there was a swimming pool just overhead. Investigation proved, however, that it was just a workman in a service area – relieving himself. We, too, were relieved," he chuckled.

Bill, Mickey, Maguis, and I visited the Anthropological Museum and the Teotihuocan pyramids while Guillermo worked. My eyes filled with tears at the old Colonial City with the Cathedral, where family members threw down blankets and jackets ahead of an ancient woman, who crawled on her bleeding knees across the rough stone patio area to the entry of the church, where she would offer her prayers. Maguis said, "This is not an isolated incident. It happens often. It is the custom."

When I admired a painting in Guillermo's study, Maguis suggested we go to visit the artist, so that I might see more of his work. The oil painting I purchased from the artist, Rafael Navarro B., is today one of my most treasured pieces of art. Leaning against a doorway and watching longingly, the painted image of a young boy in an off-white rustic peasant shirt reminds me of many of the young Chiclet salesmen I met during that visit and subsequent ones. It hangs in my tutoring room, summoning up not only memories of the day I visited the artist's studio, but also an acknowledgement of how privileged I have been. He has a kind of plaintive yearning expression on his face that one might see on a young boy, while sitting enjoying chiles rellenos in the luxury of a sidewalk café adjacent to the Zocala in Oaxaca.

After a few days, Enriqué drove us to Toluca, where we visited another home. I found the difference between these two families striking. This Senora kept everything under lock and key for fear the 'hired help' would steal from them. With a bunch of keys hanging from a belt at her waistline, she spoke of her household staff with contempt and treated them in a similar manner, as she occasionally excused herself to go and open a linen closet or the pantry for one of them. Maguis, in contrast, loved and trusted her employees, many of whom had been with them for several years.

Senor Gomez showed us around their home, explaining where each of their possessions had been purchased and how much they had paid for each. In contrast, the Ballesteros family accepted their wealth with grace. Their home, in spite of being filled with exquisite art and furnishings, felt comfortable and home-like in comparison. And it would never have occurred to them to mention money in any context. Both families, however, were very generous with their time and with offers for me to bring my family to visit as soon as it could be arranged.

Bill and Mickey were right. This proved to be not only a first-rate distraction for me, but the last time I was to spend time with my brother, who at the age of fifty-two, shortly thereafter on a business trip in Texas, died of a heart attack in his hotel room. So much sadness in our family... and in such a short time. I shared Mickey's grief. [Photo of William V. Campbell 1923-1977]

Confronting the Holidays Head On

I came to learn that turning points and plateaus are merely steps in grief – steps that lead from loss to growth. Grief is a process of gradual changes and small incremental discoveries. Each birthday, each holiday, each season, every happy or sad occasion, we all experienced what is known as 'grief work.'

To this day, over forty years later, when I hear Bridge over Troubled Waters, I celebrate a little memorial service in my mind.

We suspected the first anniversary of the fire, and its aftermath, would be the most difficult. I decided to confront the 'first' holidays – the first anniversary - head on. Determined to have them be as festive as I could make them, I asked friends of all different ages to a holiday party in mid-December with an invitation that said:

> *"Our tree will be bare,*
> *Please bring an ornament to share."*

Indeed, that night as we awaited the first ring of the doorbell, the ten-foot live potted Deodar cedar tree stood in front of the spiral stairs in our two-story entry hall, decorated only with lights. By the time the last guest arrived, the tree was brimming from top to bottom with unique ornaments. The perfect icebreaker, each guest placed their ornament on a branch before joining the party! Many of the ornaments were lovingly handmade; they each had a special meaning for us.

This party began an annual tradition that many of our friends said, "kicked off the holiday season" for them. Certainly it did for us.

The kids worked hard to help make it special for themselves and for their friends. We served my special X- and G-rated eggnogs, mulled cider and mulled wine, along with hot and cold appetizers, and because of the teen-agers and their voracious appetites, all the

49

makings for hearty sandwiches, and, of course an assortment of holiday cookies and cakes. [Photo: Our 1971 Christmas card photo taken on the spiral staircase of the new house.]

My recipe for X & G-Rated Egg Nog
Separate one dozen eggs
Beat the egg yolks until thick and light lemon color.
Add ½ pound powdered sugar and beat well.
Add 2 cups bourbon and let set for one hour.
Add 1 can of evaporated milk
½ gallon of whole milk
2 more cups of bourbon (or to taste)
Refrigerate until ready to serve, at which time:
Beat egg whites until stiff. Fold in gently just before serving.
Sprinkle with freshly grated nutmeg.
(To make G-rated Egg Nog, you simply omit the bourbon and add more milk)

Mulled Wine
1 gallon apple juice
80 cloves
6 cinnamon sticks
Rind of 4 lemons and 2 oranges
Simmer ½ hour. Remove spices and add juice of four lemons.
Add 1 gallon burgundy and a quart of port wine and heat.

After Mark joined the 16-voice Madrigal Choir from the high school, each year the group gathered at the home of the Walters, a few houses away from ours, before caroling up the street to our front door. After being greeted, they went up the stairs to our music room balcony overlooking the living room, and presented a 20-minute a cappella concert of traditional madrigal music and holiday songs. After which, Dick Brunelle, their director and pianist extraordinaire, came down and accompanied us all in carols of the season. [Mark on the far right or left in most Madrigal photos of that era, as he made a dash to his place after setting the camera.]

Wassail, Wassail!
Bring us some figgie pudding!

Christmas and New Years remained indescribably oppressive for many years, as anniversaries of deaths often are, but we prepared well for this first one.

We faced the inevitable, a holiday that would forever remind us of the tragic deaths of our husband, father, brother and son. We heeded advice I've since read in many books: Make a change in your traditions. Do something different.

We focused our change on making gifts for each other. For days before Christmas, the jigsaw, sewing machine, and darkroom buzzed with solitary activity behind closed doors, as we kept secret our surprises until the big morning.

The handmade gifts I received that first year included a wooden framed seed collage for my kitchen from Valerie, my eldest, which she created in the workshop of Dick Patrick, the architect of the medical school and one of Glen's close friends. Laurie converted a small antique washboard into a spice rack for our new kitchen. Mark busied himself in his upstairs darkroom, creating and framing several black and white photos for our upstairs hallway. Marci, always handy at the sewing machine, fashioned for me a bright orange/red robe out of three bath towels.

Our second change involved the Scott's and the Quick's. Together we rented a house at Tahoe, big enough for all of us, for the week after Christmas. We planned to be away from home on that fateful day following New Years.

Ross Quick's friend, Mark Houston mentioned to his mother, Jean, our plans for a skiing holiday, as well as for seeing a show. We didn't have any extra room at what was already expected to be a burgeoning house, but Jean was able to get reservations at a nearby motel for herself, Mark, his sister Marcia, brother Curtis, as well as Curt's two best friends, college-aged Mike Henry and Tim Magill. We secured tickets for all of us for the Andy Williams Show with the Lennon Sisters.

The Houston group added greatly to our merriment, with Jean in her exuberant way sending a note up with the maitre d', asking Andy if he would sing the Hawaiian Wedding Song. Andy replied, "Unfortunately, I can't sing that tonight, but I will sing something else especially for you." No one remembers what it was, although it was probably what he'd intended to sing all along. But that's not the important part of the story.

Aside from Mark, we had not met any of the Houston party until that night at the casino, but they were an easy group to get to know. We enjoyed the show together and invited them to join us the next day for breakfast, fun and games. And that's when the real story began.

Valerie, home for her winter holiday from Reed College, especially enjoyed the good-natured camaraderie of Mike, Curt, and Tim, as they played bridge to while away the next afternoon. Valerie, who had been isolated by her back pain and surgeries, had not dated in high school or, to my knowledge, much in college either.

Jean planned to drive back to Davis that afternoon, but it was soon decided that there would be plenty of room for the boys to bed down on the floor in their sleeping bags at our rented house that next night. Everyone was having too much fun it seemed to break up the group. The following day, Valerie decided to ride back to Davis with Mike, Tim and Curt – a day early, so that she "could work on a term paper."

I almost believed that story then. Later I figured out that she was enjoying this contemporary male companionship far more than she was letting on.

Several days later, Valerie went back to school. Tim became a great friend to the whole family, stopping by on a regular basis. It seemed somewhat obvious that Mike, however, came by only when he suspected Valerie would be home for a break from college. She and Mike began to date whenever she was home for a vacation, so I was not surprised when that spring she decided to transfer to UC Davis for her final year. Ostensibly, so that she would be able to study a more practical application of math, not to waste more time on the theoretical that would be required if she were to write the required thesis to graduate from Reed.

Or so her rationale went. However, I didn't just fall off the turnip truck! I suspected other motives.

At at the game table: Natalie Nickerson, Kristin Cooper, Ross Quick, Laurie and Dave Scott.

Back to Reality

I've always taken pride in being able to teach myself new things, usually through total immersion, reading everything I can find about my current interest. I taught myself to type when I was ten years old and did clerical chores in my mother's insurance office during my pre-teen and teen years. This early training enabled me to get a summer job as an insurance actuary right out of high school. It later provided me with the chutzpah to apply for jobs for which I had no previous training or background.

We were now moved into the new house and I guess finally, almost a year later, had the time and, perhaps, the concentration to seek answers to this emotional turmoil. When could I expect to feel normal? What is this thing called "grief work?" And how does one do it?

It was at this time that I studied everything I could find on grief and bereavement, although there wasn't much available at that time. From Elisabeth Kubler-Ross's classic, *On Death and Dying*, I was both relieved and distressed to learn that grief is like the ebb and flowing of the tide and that it varies from person to person and is not a set-in-stone process. Aside from outlining the stages of grief, that book did not seem to address my needs of how to weather the storm after a sudden death. Next I read Lynn Caine's book, *Widow*, in which she mentioned a support group.

Now that sounded like something that might help me through this difficult time – someone with whom to share coping skills, a place to talk with people who might really understand. There was nothing like this in Davis.

Since childhood, I'd been brainwashed by all the old songs like 'You're Nobody Until Somebody Loves You' and 'I'd sacrifice anything come what might, For the sake of havin' you near', from Cole Porter's, 'I've Got You Under My Skin', and the more recent, 'As Long As He Needs Me'. Love is a fundamental teaching – a moral imperative even. It conquers all. Without the love of a man, am I still of value? Until now, I had believed those songs and others I'd grown up hearing. I hadn't a clue about exactly who I was, but I was determined to find out. This time of grief, this time of extreme loss, was my search for meaning. I longed to find my center, to explore who I was at my core. I knew that it seemed bad form to feel sad, angry, or guilty. I believed that no one wanted to hear my feelings unless they were positive, upbeat ones.

We live in a culture where people greet each other with "Hello, how are you?" "Fine, thanks, and you?" Never mind that you are in great pain or distraught because you've just found you have a dread disease or your best friend has died. Fake it! Remember our role models, Jacqueline Kennedy and Mrs. King.

People were still telling Mark, "Be brave. You're the man of the family now," and I was still saying, "He's just a boy."

Just a month after the fire, a letter came for Mark from Dr. Reed Nesbitt, the elder statesman of the Medical School. It enumerated the classic prerequisites of a good physician and encouraged him to 'choose this noble profession for, if you do, you will find enjoyment and stimulation from your day of commitment, until the end of your enjoyable and rewarding career.' He heard from yet others: "You should go to medical school, Mark. That would make your Dad proud."

I knew that what would have made his dad most proud related to Mark – to all of his children - being a happy, healthy, well-adjusted human being, doing something challenging that he enjoyed. Not necessarily medical school, unless that was something he really wanted.

I received from a friend, at a time when I was deeply depressed, an anonymous quote that has been an inspiration to me: 'Our only real security in life is our ability to change.' I substitute the word "adapt" for change, and it works for me.

Another quote from some very significant reading I did in my search for meaning came from Viktor Frankl's *Man's Search for Meaning*: 'We who've lived in a concentration camp can remember the men who walked through the huts comforting others, giving away their last pieces of bread. They offered proof that anything can be taken from man but the last of the human freedoms; to choose one's attitude in any set of circumstances, to choose one's own way."

Ah! I can choose how to think about things. A choice.

Every loss, large or small, can be made an opportunity for growth. How we deal with the little losses is very likely how we are going to deal with the big ones. I didn't choose what happened to my family, but I'm stuck with it. Now what can I do with what fate dealt us?

What we do matters. What actions you take matters. The choices you make count. What was it that Gram used to tell me? "It's an ill wind, indeed, Joni, that blows no good at all." Today, people say "If life gives you lemons, make lemonade." I've got to dig myself out of the doldrums and make something of my life. Make a commitment to life.

I began to yearn for adult company. I could always count on Dick and Shipley Walters to invite me over for 'adult hour,' and with them, I could be myself. And there was the occasional invitation to a party at Judy and Andy Gabor's or Phyllis and Bob Bolt's. I remember after one such occasion, telling Phyllis Bolt how much I appreciated their including me; how few and far between those invitations now seemed to come. Phyll, in her wisdom, asked, "Maybe people don't know you're ready to socialize, Joan. When did you last have a party, except your Christmas Open House? When did you last invite a small group to dinner?"

That was a good question. Aside from the kids and their friends – my constant companions – I hadn't entertained at all. Truth be told, I didn't feel worthy of anyone else's company.

About that time, either that day or the next, Sunset Magazine, featuring an article on a Walk-Around Dinner Party, arrived in my mailbox. It seemed almost serendipitous, coming as it had right after my conversation with Phyllis. I began to write the invitations. My plan was to invite not only my friends from the old days, but my children's friends, as well. I knew I was comfortable with them.

No tables to set, no place cards, no seating arrangements, no formality – just my cup of tea these days. Neither a cocktail party nor a dinner party – a walk-around party! A perfect solution for the hostess who is entertaining for the first time without a host.

All kinds of beverages with hot and cold canapés greeted our guests of all ages, who could then wander around through stations set up inside and outside the house. They could start with a choice of chilled soup, situated outside the pass-through window from the kitchen, or enjoy their 'salad' with crudités served with dips in hollowed out cabbages, and fruit and cheese from a table on the patio – an invitation to summer. Festive!

In the kitchen, a rib roast, turning on the Jenn-Air spit, emitted a succulent smell, portent of things to come. Several sauces, horseradish, mayonnaise and mustards accompanied the sliced beef, turkey, and ham, for make-it-yourself walk-around potato-roll sandwiches.

No last minute cooking and no serving, just guests mingling and walking about. And having the teen-age and college ages there to mix with the older crowd turned out to be perfect for a first party.

The dining table served as a display for a variety of desserts; the pièce de résistance a strawberry-kiwi Pavlova I'd learned how to make under the directions of Kate Morice, a young woman visiting from New Zealand.

A walk-around dinner provided the ideal setting for me to relax and enjoy the company of guests of all ages. It proved that entertaining isn't only about well-planned, elaborate, multi-course sit-down dinner, complete with seating arrangements and place cards. This low-keyed get-together ranks high on the list of parties I've ever given – my first, flying solo, one of the scariest to even contemplate, but it became one of my most successful.

Pavlova a la Morice
    3 large or 4 small egg whites
    1 ¼ c. sugar
    3 T. cold water
    Pinch of salt
    ½ tsp. Vanilla
    1 T. vinegar
    3 tsp. Cornstarch

1. Beat the egg whites until they begin to peak. Gradually add sugar and water alternately one tablespoon at a time. Then add salt, vanilla, and vinegar. Fold in the cornstarch.

2. Mound on buttered foil on pan. Bake at 275 degrees for one hour and then turn oven off and leave it in the cooling oven for another hour.

3. Garnish with lightly sweetened whipped cream (to which you've added a bit of plain gelatin in a small quantity of water), strawberries or kiwi (or both). Refrigerate until ready to serve.

Centering

Within us lives a merciful being who helps us to our feet however many times we fall.
-M. C. Richards - *Centering*

I quit my job as a legal secretary at the time of the fire. I worried and wondered if I would ever be able to hold a job again, as my memory continued to fail me and concentration seemed impossible. I didn't know that it was a normal and natural part of the second stage of grief and feared it would never improve, although my doctor friends assured me that it would.

I did an inventory of my capabilities as honestly as I knew how - and my self-appraisal surprised me. First, I discovered that I had gone through my whole life being what others wanted me to be, doing what gained for me the most acceptance and love.

What a revelation! All my life I have accepted someone else's expectations and values as my own, without much exploration or evaluation.

When tragedy struck, even then I sought approval. Everyone commented on how brave and controlled I was. They approved. Everyone admires the bereaved who hide their grief so fully that no one would ever guess what happened – a performance so that others will not be discomfited by the obvious distress of those experiencing the grief.

I finally decided after beating myself up for several months: I have a number of skills, if I can just get over the memory lapses. Over the past twenty years, I've been an administrative assistant and speechwriter at the University and worked as a medical transcriptionist, as well as most recently a legal secretary. I've got a logical mind when I can get it to work properly; I'm an accurate, fast typist, and I have enough organizational skills to run this high-energy outfit we call a family! Surely that's marketable, even without a perfect memory.

Everyone says that every grief is unique. My grief prompted me to take a close look at myself. I did a lot of introspection and ultimately found the strength and independence of spirit I needed to survive emotionally. I took some stitchery classes and made quilts. I volunteered on Jerome Waldie's unsuccessful gubernatorial political campaign. I made a conscious choice that I couldn't go through the rest of my life feeling sorry for myself. I didn't want to fall apart; I wanted to be happy.

JOAN SNODGRASS, secretary of Citizens for Waldie, shows Lee Sheldon, co-chairman, the quilt she designed and she and others made to help benefit the Jerome Waldie campaign fund. The quilt, which has a blue and gold UCD motif, will be on display in the Waldie booth at the Yolo county fair. (Staff photo)

This is going to force me to survive on my own, to find out how I want to survive, and what I want to do with my life. I surely don't want someone to take care of me and make my decisions for me. I have children who need me. I need to do more than survive.

About this time my neighbor, Merry Burns, and I sat drinking a glass of wine one night, pondering what we were going to do with the rest of our lives. Her husband had also recently died at a young age. We decided to try Real Estate School, believing we could help people find their perfect house. We had an eye for that sort of thing. But alas! The very first class turned us off. That's not what we want to do. Not at all! That sounded really boring – and much more demanding of our weekend time than we thought would be good for our families.

I remember asking a "Why" question at that first class and being told, "You don't need to know why. Your broker will know the whys." Well, I always have to know why! We never went back.

Not long ago a young woman called and asked if she could come by and 'pick my brains' about opening a women's clothing store in Davis. I was at once enchanted and amused by her enthusiasm and naiveté. It reminded me of a time that Merry and I, both young widows, just forty years old, each with teen-aged children, still searching for what to do with our lives, dreamed of opening a store.

Merry did a lot of traveling and I'd done little. But a cursory inventory showed that between us we had many skills and talents – enough to find opening a small shop, an art gallery perhaps, not only feasible, but also an exciting possibility. Neither Merry nor I were dependent on an income from this venture, what we hoped for was something to help us make a life, not a livelihood.

We immediately started traveling up and down the state, stopping at every Art Co-Op, getting to know artists and artisans, lining them up for showing their things in our gallery on a consignment basis. In the meantime, we rented a small space across the street from the U. S. Post Office and near Davis Lumber and Hardware, two active destinations.

We thought this new building, with its beauty salon, small deli-type restaurant, yarn shop, and art cooperative would provide synergy conducive to a thriving new business – ours!

Next we decided on décor: We paneled one wall with pecky cedar (to which I soon discovered I was allergic, although happily, it was just a contact-dermatitis type allergy that went away as soon as I stopped nailing up the siding.) We also designed cubicle display cases, also of pecky cedar, similar to some we'd seen at a flea market. They could be arranged in a variety of configurations and easily changed to fit pottery pieces of varying heights and widths. The cubicles could be viewed from both sides, giving maximum display space in this small 800 square foot shop.

I had recently read the book, *Centering,* by M. C. Richards, in which she says, "Wisdom arrives through a childlike sense of wonder, or through centering. Within us lives a merciful being," she observes, "who helps us to our feet however many times we fall."

Merry and I had each experienced a serious fall. We were searching for that inner merciful being.

Richards encourages her readers to "Ride our lives like natural beasts, like tempests, like the bounce of a ball or the slightest ambiguous hovering of ash, the drift of scent...."

Since we hoped to feature pottery in our store, and since "centering" is an integral part of throwing a pot, I suggested the name for our store. Centering in life is the opposite of "torn-to-pieces-hood", from which Merry and I hoped to recover. It seemed the perfect name.

In our travels, we met an artist and art dealer in Sacramento, who introduced us to some other artists who were willing to put their serigraphs in our gallery on consignment. We found some exquisite pottery, as well as more whimsical pieces, many of which I still own, never being able to part with them in the end. I always said that I have more of Gregg Moll's pottery than even his mother.

Another dealer introduced us to Hundertwasser. We featured his sixteen-color silkscreens with metal imprints in five colors on metallic cardboard, some in the original frames he had designed for a show in Japan. While Davis wasn't quite ready for art of this caliber (read "price"), Merry and I both made purchases, which we still enjoy. I always told our clients, "Buy art because you love it, not because it's a good investment or because it coordinates with your color-scheme." Rainy Day on the Regentag fit all three of these concepts. It is still one of my favorites.

A more financially successful show featured the sepia toned photos of Geronimo, Chief Joseph, Medicine Crow and others, by E.

S. Curtis or "Shadow Catcher", as he was called by some of the Indian tribes he captured in photos.

As it turned out, Merry really enjoyed the setting up and the creative part of starting a store, the day to day operations less so. As I did the bookkeeping, much of the buying, and writing and placing advertising, I found it fascinating and challenging. I even enjoyed working in the store and chatting with customers (when we had them). Some days were very quiet in the beginning. [Photo: Merry Dean Burns at a Centering Opening]

Merry found other avenues of more interest to her than working in the store during these quiet times, so I offered to buy her out. One of the brilliant things we had done as we started the partnership was to have Attorney Roger Gambatese draw up an agreement, a ready-made plan for exactly how disassociation would be handled.

We had been sharing the time working in the store, so my new independence meant much less in many ways. I hired some part-time student help – a series of wonderful people, who contributed in a variety of ways. One young woman, a design student, arrived for her shift in a different costume each day. She did outrageous things, so "People won't look through me. I hate walking down the street as though I'm invisible." One day she arrived dressed as a mud puddle – an outfit made of double sheets of heavy-duty plastic with mud between them. I dare say people must have noticed her!

Every day Phyllis Beals, another one of my student employees, wore a different hat, some of which she designed and constructed. She later sold her hats to a clientele of the rich and famous.

These students brought new life to my dream.

What started out as an art gallery, with some pottery, gradually evolved as my passion for ethnic art took over. It became obvious that in order to make the store profitable, I would need to go to the Gift Show in San Francisco and Los Angeles to find saleable merchandise to supplement the art, which while enjoying a viewing audience did not provide a solid customer base. I began to bring in African art, and then just whatever caught my eye at market.

One day one of my student helpers noticed, on her way to work, a bead shop that was closed and with a "For Sale" sign on the window. When she inquired, she said she was told "The owner, a woman with a small child, had a premonition that California is going to be stricken with a horrific earthquake. So she abandoned her business – escaped. And it's up for sale now."

This was the 70's. Beads and jewelry making were in vogue. Certainly Davis, a college town, needed a bead shop. So I bought her inventory and a couple of her glass-fronted bead cases for a pittance, and soon shopped to supplement her inventory. Strands of puka shells, tiger-eye, turquoise, lapis lazuli, coral, and several other gemstones now hung on pegs behind the glass cases.

I continued to add to the original supply. I bought a scale and liquid silver in bulk, as it was the hot item for jewelry at the time. We measured it out into little bags and sold all the fixin's for earrings of all kinds, as well as clasps for necklaces for men and women. We displayed individual beads of all kinds and from all countries in small ceramic dishes of different colors; each marked with price and a brief description.

Wooden hand-carved bead boards made it easy for people to see their creations before making their purchases. While this brought a lot of people into the store, it required at least two staff to show the beads, put them away, and keep the place stocked and in order.

One day at market, I met Laurel Burch, who designed jewelry, primarily silver and gold pressed metal earrings, but with a few cloisonné enamel earrings produced in China. She later expanded into clothing, dishes, and cards. Laurel, a single mother, had up until this time, been a street vendor in San Francisco, designing one-of-kind necklaces and earrings, and selling them on the street to support herself and her two children.

I first bought some Laurel Burch silver and gold colored pressed metal earrings, Egyptian in theme, unusual for our time and very expensive. They would retail for between $12 and $16! I didn't have room for more than a few pair at a time, because of the bead display - or confidence because of the price of these newfound baubles.

I was in for a surprise. These and even more expensive enameled earrings flew out of the store. I couldn't keep them in stock. I phoned in a new order every couple of days. (Very expensive? Within a few years, I would be selling earrings for ten times that much – and more! Who would have believed it back in those early days?)

It didn't take a rocket scientist to decide that one could sell six pair of Laurel Burch earrings in the same time it took to help a bead customer put together a necklace with supplies worth $2.55! So one night the beads disappeared and the cases became filled with Laurel Burch and Thousand Flower earrings, and all things bright and beautiful.

My *passion for accessories began! And the dream continued to evolve.*

So what do I tell this young woman who has a dream? I guess I tell her to follow her dream and just show up. Just like M. C.

Richards said, the imagination, inspiration, intuition, all the fabulous functioning of this human being you are will take you to places you haven't yet dreamed. I guess that's my story. I followed it day by day – and I showed up. Centering was the first step in helping me get centered again.

My suggestion to my new young friend: Dream your dream, show up – **and make a business plan!**

Kim McKnight and me

Bereavement Outreach

Perhaps, just perhaps,
something you have done,
have left behind,
has endured, influenced,
or added something of value in another's life.
                                    -Rick Storey.

When I first knew grief, I wasn't sure I would live through it, or that I even wanted to. But from that great stress I know now that I gained strength. The following six years turned out to be the greatest growth period of my adult life. I found strengths I hadn't known I had. My reading led me to record in my journal some quotes for me to live by. From Dostoyevsky: "There is only one thing that I dread, and that is not to be worthy of my suffering." I silently added, "...and for that of my husband and son."

One night at dinner, Mark dropped this little blockbuster; "Val and Marci are both off at college and Laurie will be going soon. I think I'll just go to UC Davis and live at home, Mom. Then you won't be all alone."

It was true I'd enjoyed the companionship of the girls and all their friends – so much so, in fact, that I hadn't made much of an effort to expand my own circle of friends. Not that I couldn't have, if I had wanted to, mind you, but I had just become content and complacent. What I knew that I did not want was a forty-five-year old son still living at home with Mama one day. Yikes!

Mark's pronouncement led me to the conclusion that maybe I needed to go out more, to dissuade him of the notion I couldn't function by myself. As a symbol of moving into this new realm, I took off my rings and put them in the hands of a creative jeweler at the Gold Lion in downtown Davis. He melted down the gold and formed the rings into a teardrop pendant with the engagement ring diamond in the center. I have worn it on a chain around my neck every day since then.

When an article promoting a new singles group appeared in the Davis Enterprise a few days later, it seemed serendipitous. I gave myself permission to go to the first meeting of New Dimensions for

Ecumenical Singles because a casual friend, psychologist Hanna Bauer, was speaking.

It's at a church and I know Hannah. It surely won't be like that other singles group I've heard so much about. That one seems just too threatening – I've even heard they throw their house keys in the middle of the floor!

Dr. Bauer divided us into groups and gave each of us a paperclip, which we were invited to form into a shape that represented something about ourselves. I remember that I unfolded the fastener and then tried to restore it to its original state. When asked to tell my story, I told how, just like my paperclip, I experienced trauma and would never again be exactly as I had been before – that I was gradually taking on a new way of thinking and of being.

At that first meeting, I met two people who would change my life, one for a short time and one forever. The first one, Louise Wilson, a young widow like me, was studying at Sacramento State University to become a therapist. She and I talked about the new book *Widow*, which we had each just read. We both wished for a Widow-to-Widow program such as the one Lynn Caine described and pondered the idea of starting one of our own.

Louise and I agreed to meet again to think about what a program might look like. In the meantime, I met with Dr. Herbert Bauer and his wife Hannah, Co-Presidents of the Mental Health Association of Yolo County (MHAYC), and their board. They welcomed the idea of our starting such a program under the umbrella of that non-profit agency. There was no shortage of widowed people who yearned for a supportive network. In fact, we broadened the scope to include anyone who'd suffered a loss through death, not just those who were widowed.

We designed a program we called Bereavement Outreach, in which those who had suffered the death of a loved one got together on a regular basis to talk about their losses and to support one another. It was hugely successful and over the months grew to include both men and women, who suffered losses in a variety of ways: deaths due to long illnesses, as well as sudden deaths and suicide of spouses, parents, and children.

We were surprised, and somewhat disconcerted, when some of the people, mostly women, seeking support with the group had been widowed for ten or more years. While these women expressed the belief that they had long ago completed the fifth stage of grief of which Kubler-Ross wrote in On Death and Dying – acceptance, many admitted to feeling stuck, unable to move beyond "widowhood." One woman confessed that she never made a purchase without thinking whether her long-deceased husband would have approved. Another had not driven on the freeway in the eight years since her husband had died. One man had not yet removed his late wife's clothing from their closet or her make-up from her dressing table, although he declared interest in finding someone with whom he might share his remaining years.

My own experience, substantiated by that which I observed of the many participants of Bereavement Outreach over the five years I facilitated the group, convinced me that the real grief work begins after the five stages identified by most in the literature: Shock, Denial, Anger, Depression, and Acceptance.

Few of the participants in the Bereavement Outreach program thought of themselves as angry, saying, "Oh, I went through that angry stage awhile ago." Through discussions within the group, it became apparent that anger still lived within many, albeit unfocused and perhaps in unrecognizable forms. Thinly veiled signs remained however in statements, such as: "I'm not angry – I'm just disappointed. We had planned…" "If only he had… (Fill in the blank - eaten healthier, smoked less, and exercised more…)." Some laughed or grinned, often using humor to hide their feelings of impotence and sometimes rage that seethed just below the surface. Others seemed indifferent, although acknowledging that they were often accused of being condescending, critical, and annoyed with their children or friends. They admitted that they often got exasperated at small things. These behaviors along with becoming isolated and withdrawn can all be symptoms of anger.

Negative language was also a dead giveaway that anger still lingered. Words like "bitter," "disappointed," "deserve," "should," and "if only" cropped up with great frequency in Bereavement Outreach meetings. Unfulfilled expectations can act as a catalyst for feelings of self-pity and victimization, which indicated that guilt and resentment had not yet been successfully worked through.

Facing the reality of what loss means to you and your life is the easiest part. Working through the full range of emotions and reorganizing your life, coping with lifestyle changes, rebuilding social relations and feeling connected to others may be a bit more complicated. This is where the grief work comes in. As Anne Morrow Lindbergh wrote, your need for courage isn't just for the moment you experience the loss, "…but for the long uphill battle to faith, sanity, and security." The experiences of the Bereavement Outreach participants proved to us that there is no direct route to healing. We must each deal with losses in our own way and at our own pace, recognizing that there will be ups and downs and that as age-old wisdom says, time can be your best friend or your worst enemy.

The focus of conversation varied from week to week with new members invited to tell the story of their loss; the rest of the group listened, contributing, sharing experiences, or asking questions to help provide clarity. An issue that came up time and time again involved comments like: "Everyone thinks I should be over it by now." "It's as though he never existed – no one mentions his name." The bereaved universally expressed feelings of isolation.

As a group we talked about how friends and family might ease those feelings. Some of their ideas include:

Do be patient.

Do let me talk when I need to or want to

Be a sounding board

Don't offer quick fixes; help me look at options rather than give me advice.

Call me. Don't say "If there's anything you need, just call me," because when I really need you, I won't have the confidence or audacity to call when I most need you

Don't forget me. I really need you.

Be available; please don't stay away

Don't be afraid to talk about the loss with me.

Don't try to distract me with forced cheerfulness.

Anesthetizing with alcohol or drugs just prolongs the grief.

Use the name of the person who has died

Talk with me about shared memories

It's okay to laugh.

Remember me at birthdays, anniversaries and holidays – those are the hardest times sometimes for years to come.

We discovered that a big component of the grief process often involved overcoming fear, as well as guilt and anger – fear of developing new skills or roles, perhaps not required before; fear of new relationships with the world; life style changes, new independence; as well as new identity. Will I ever get over it? Who am

I now? I'm so forgetful? I can't concentrate. I feel such deep sadness. How can I go on? How will I ever be able to move past this? What will my future be like?

We also discovered that how we had learned to deal with little losses determined to a great degree how we would deal with bigger ones. I remember how irritated I felt when an acquaintance said, "Joan, you're young. You'll marry again." Before I opened my mouth though, I remembered how our beloved Keeshond Roby had died unexpectedly and mysteriously in a kennel where we had boarded her when we first moved to New Orleans several years ago. I realize now that we had not allowed our children to grieve. We had quickly found another Keeshond and had it shipped from Ohio, almost before the children had become aware of Roby's death. I now know that was a mistake. We sheltered our children from a learning experience – from the sadness and despair that death can bring. Nothing, of course, could have prepared them for the loss at the death of their father and brother, but another pet arriving so quickly after the first one died prevented them from having their first experience of grief.

Just as I was told, "You'll marry again," couples who experience a miscarriage in the early months of pregnancy are often told, "Your chance of a subsequent successful pregnancy is good." It is perfectly normal for the couple to experience significant grief and despair, but friends and family may not even yet have been made aware of the pregnancy, and therefore may not feel any sense of loss. The couple grieve alone or are told, "You'll get pregnant again," while often self-blaming with, "Did I do something wrong?"

Because each person's grief is different, the husband and wife may not experience the death of a child or a miscarriage in an equal way. Men and women from childhood are often taught to handle their feelings differently. Generally, masculine grief tends to be private, sometimes action-oriented rather than thinking and feeling. It is important that family members be tolerant of the different approaches that other family members may take. Few people can understand how deeply a bereaved parent hurts unless they have been there.

Together, Louise and I developed a graphic diagram, The Grief Process: Turning Points for Growth, which synthesized the ideas from our general research of the literature on grief.

Louise facilitated the group until she moved to Southern California a few months later. I took up where she left off. It was rewarding in more ways than one. While helping others to work through their grief, I worked through my own.

I gave talks on an abbreviated version of *It's An Ill Wind Indeed*... throughout the state and helped others start Bereavement

Outreach programs in their communities. This became an important part of my life and accelerated my own grief process and was probably the greatest growth period in my adult life. I became much more confident. Public speaking became easier for me with this topic, on which I had unwittingly become an authority.

THE GRIEF PROCESS: TURNING POINT for GROWTH

Loss →   Growth →

Third Phase

- regained energy
- relief from somatic symptoms
- renewed interest in life
- new goals for the future
- increased self-confidence

Reorganization

•accomodation to loss
• renewed hope and optimism

• shock
• disbelief
• denial
• anger
• self-recrimination

(FEELINGS)

• despair
• apathy
• depression
• social isolation
• meaninglessness
• hopelessness
• self-doubt

Intense Grief

Shock and Protest

First Phase

-crying
-weeping/sobbing
-searching
-sighing
-somatic symptoms
  tightness in the chest
  loss of appetite
  sleep disturbance
  muscle weakness

Second Phase

-continued somatic symptoms
-restlessness
-poor memory and lack of concentration
- loss of interest in activity apart from grieving
- loss of energy

Note: This diagram is a synthesis of ideas from the general research literature on grief, but specific aspects have been drawn from the work of Wm. Lamers, C. M. Parkes, and s. Keleman

And Simultaneously...

That other important person I met at that first meeting of New Dimensions, Ed Callaway, became a good friend. That same night when plans started to be made for the next meeting, I volunteered my home; Ed offered to help with refreshments and to set up chairs or whatever was needed.

I soon learned that he had custody of his adopted eleven-year-old daughter, Shelley, who, typically pre-adolescent, challenged his good humor on an almost daily basis. We shared many of our trials and troubles from then on.

I was immediately attracted to his easy smiling good looks and his compassionate good-natured gentleness. Too bad things are as they are! Ten years younger than I, he probably dates girls my eldest daughter's age!

Oh, well! I enjoyed his company, and when I perceived one of the husbands of my social group a bit too affectionate, Ed became the ideal 'date' to take along to dinner and cocktail parties. This discouraged unwelcome attentions.

Let them think we were an item!

I cringed a bit when I saw him at Berkeley Repertory Theatre with a young woman, or when he told me about a trip they had taken to the Grand Canyon in a rented airplane he'd just learned to fly. Never mind that I might be with a date, myself, or have just returned from a trip somewhere! Our platonic friendship continued and grew, even as we both dated other people, never even dreaming of the possibility of each other as anything other than good friends.

Well, maybe I dreamed a little, but not seriously. He's too young – or I'm too old, whichever. But my relationship with Ed reminds me of a quote – maybe Elizabeth Barrett Browning – "I love you not only for who you are, but for who I am when I am with you."

And this was then - 1974

No Man Is an Island

For a long time I was certain that the wrong one of us survived. Glen had been an innovative administrator for the new medical school, a community organizer, a great father, husband and lover - and at 39, just in his prime. As Rev. Senghas said in his eulogy, "'Greater love has no man, than this, that a man lay down his life for his friends.' That is how Glen lived, and that is how he died. More than that is not possible for any man, that in death he celebrated the value of life in its ultimate form."

Me? I wasn't even being a very good mother these days, much less making a contribution to my community. I began to think that I'd better find that good the ill wind did blow -- make something of myself; be worthy.

For the past twenty years, off and on with no apparent cause, I'd been plagued with trigeminal neuralgia, commonly known as 'tic douloureux'. This disorder of the fifth cranial nerve causes episodes of intense, stabbing, electric shock-like pain in the areas around the lips, eyes, nose, scalp, forehead, and upper and lower jaw. Something as simple as brushing my teeth or even a slight breeze or the sheet brushing up against my face could set off an attack, resulting in moments of agony. Attacks sometimes lasted for hours, other times for weeks, or intermittently – or, blessedly, an occasional remission for several months.

One day I got a call from Dr. Benner, who continued to be my doctor, taking care of me as he had promised Glen, "Joan, there's a doctor back in Cincinnati performing high frequency blockage of the nerve. He's successfully removing the pain without causing any cosmetic alteration of the face. I think you should give it a try."

With my permission, he sent my records to the doctor, who agreed I sounded like a good candidate for the procedure. I headed for Cincinnati with little preparation of how this might affect me emotionally when, after the procedure, I experienced complete numbness in the right side of my face, much like that which is produced by Novocaine at the dentist's office.

My sister-in-law, who lived in Seattle, ignored my "Oh, no, Mickey. I'll be fine. I don't need anyone to go with me," and met me at the hotel where I would be staying both before and, for a couple of days, after the procedure. If I thought I'd been depressed before, it was nothing compared to what I experienced immediately after, when the numbness was at its most intense. My speech felt slurred, I constantly bit the inside of my mouth, and had to resort to chewing food only on the left side. And worse yet, I felt as though my appearance changed and that people could see the numbness – of course, they couldn't. Over the next few weeks this outcome subsided some, although never completely.

I was more than a little grateful that my late brother's wife, Mickey, ignored my assertions of independence. This proved yet another time when isolation would have been a drastic mistake. What is it they say? "No man is an island?" Why is it so difficult for me to admit I need other people?

Turn Around, Turn Around

After graduating from U. C. Davis, Valerie started law school in Sacramento – briefly. Mike, finished with graduate school, took a job as Grounds Superintendent at Del Mesa Carmel. They soon tired of this long-distance romance. So, instead of our regular Christmas party that year, we had a wedding at Newman Center and a reception at our home on the 15th of December.

I shed a few tears before we left for the church. My thoughts turned to how Glen would have loved to be there, to see Valerie moving on in her life and how well she had grown up.

In spite of the little memorial service in my mind, I don't believe I've ever been to a wedding and reception more fun than this one. When we arrived in front of the chapel, we noticed guests pointing at something on the lawn and laughing. What could it be?

This brings us to a whole other story, but to be brief: A year or so before, I had received a gift of one of those plastic pink flamingos. I laughingly told the 6:30 a.m. surprise birthday party group that the Elmwood Protective Association would be after me if I planted that in our yard. One thing led to another and it became an object that got passed around - first with one of its leg wrapped with a bandage to a friend who had a broken leg. It soon became a birthday tradition, once sent to one of Mark's friends with a "singing telegram." It had recently gone to Jan Furman, whose landlady had been so impressed, she added additional charm. Jan arrived early and had carefully placed the pink flamingo, along with its new entourage of white ducklings at the entrance to Newman Chapel. That was to be the first of many surprises at this wedding – fully appreciated by all the past recipients of the 'gift' that had over time been presented in ever-more challenging and creative ways.

The ceremony was a traditional Catholic wedding with Grandpa Jack giving the bride away. Dick Walters and his daughter Leslie sang a duet - "Turn Around" - sure to bring a tear to the eye of any parent whose daughter is getting married. Best Man Tim Magill drove the newlyweds away from the church to the reception at our home in the rumble seat of his creamy yellow Model T. [Photo: My mother, Bea Adams, Me, Marci, Laurie and Valerie as we head out the door on our way to Newman Chapel.]

Where are you goin' my little one, little one?
Where are you goin' my baby my own?

Fearing that his unruly friends might do something outrageous to his car, Mike made arrangements to hide it earlier in the day in the garage of our friends Bob and Joyce Wisner, who live in a small cul-de-sac down at the end of our large circle street. In true counter-subterfuge, Tim drove them away from the reception, out of Elmwood Drive and around the block a few times in an effort to escape the friends they were sure would follow. At the same time, he was also a part of the conspiracy. The extra turn around town gave close friends and family time to gather and walk down to the Wisner's, secrete

79

themselves in the garage, and get ready to surprise the newlyweds once again – the car, of course, adorned by the 'unruly friends' appropriate to the occasion.

Valerie later described the next morning when the valet at their S. F. hotel delivered their car to them. A bus full of tourists, who were unloading, looked on, laughing and making rude comments, enjoying the embarrassment of the blushing couple.

They made their first home in Monterey where Mike worked for some time. From there, they moved to Santa Ana, when Mike took a job with University Extension as a Farm Advisor, specializing in turf management. It was there that Lisa Danielle Henry was born, prematurely at 3lb. 3 oz. by Caesarian section. She remained in the hospital for about a month with Valerie pumping breast milk and delivering it to the hospital on her daily visits.

Another turning point…

The Elephant in the Room

I gradually found myself depressed less and less often, no more than what would be considered usual with life's normal events. Oh, I had the occasional intermittent little memorial services in my mind at trigger events, such as when I'd see a little guy peddling by on his bike, wearing a Scout uniform or on his way to a Little League game. The holidays, and special milestone events, continued to be difficult times for the whole family, but I had increased confidence in myself. If the toilet overflowed, I didn't sit down and add to the water supply with my tears. I could handle everyday life again.

When Marci wasn't doing handstands and flips with her friends, she could probably be found with her group of girl friends or Tim McCorkle, who was a constant friend from junior high through high school. Tim went to college at Cal Poly, while Marci lived in the dorm and attended the University of California in Davis. While I liked Tim, I hoped Marci would open herself to dating other young men while at college.

In retrospect, I find it interesting that I would feel that way, given the fact that Glen and I dated each other exclusively from our junior year in high school until our marriage in our second year of college.

Marci lived on campus her first year and in an apartment her second. From a mother's perspective, she came home primarily to launder her clothes and use the oven for baking for her friends, or to give an occasional pool party.

There are economic benefits for a child to go to college in her hometown, and, in our case, emotional benefits, as well. But in contrast to Valerie's homecomings from Reed in Portland, I think Marci missed the little bit of homesickness that comes with that first quarter of college; the excitement that is felt at each vacation - Thanksgiving, Christmas and spring break. I'm sure I did.

Laurie, a JV cheerleader in her sophomore year at the time of the fire, went through the motions that year. She says now, "High school was a holding pattern for all intents and purposes. I backed off from relationships because I felt too different, and normal experiences seemed too unreal and unimportant. In some ways everything was just a pretense until I discovered modern dance that same year." She continued her interest in gymnastics, partially because of her exuberant and fun-loving coach, Jan Furman, but toward the end of her sophomore year, Laurie found her niche in modern dance. She still always seemed to find time to swim, getting up each morning before school and doing at least a few laps across our backyard pool or going with Dave Scott for early morning swimming workouts.

If there is such a thing as middle child syndrome, Laurie exhibited it from the time Mark was born when she was almost two years old. It is said that the middle child or children often have a sense of not belonging or of not being seen. They fight to receive attention from parents and others because they often feel they are being ignored or identified as being the same as another sibling. Even as a young child Laurie looked for direction from her older sisters, often acting as though she felt out of place and insecure. This continued into her pre-adolescent years, as well, when mornings often turned into a nightmare, as she tried on outfit after outfit, with nothing suiting her mood of the day. This beautiful girl repeatedly said, "I feel so ugly."

We were relieved when she came home after a summer camp experience when she was just twelve, feeling renewed and exhilarated. When I went to pick her up, as the bus delivered her back to Davis, imagine my surprise to hear girls from every window yelling, "Bye, Buggerweed! See ya later, Buggerweed!" I was even more surprised to hear her yell back some friendly greeting. It seemed to me that her counselor had taken a big risk by introducing Laurie, "You'll never believe it, Girls, but we have someone in our group named "Buggerweed." It could have been disastrous. Instead, Laurie rose to the occasion and accepted it with grace, and her campmates respected and admired her for it. She seemed like a new person. She'd obviously had a great time, in spite of my worrying two weeks earlier, as she boarded the bus with no friend or sister for company.

Snodgrass is a name our kids have learned to live with, as it has always been an easy name to ridicule. It was only when each child came to the realization that there are not many Snodgrass's in the telephone book, they decided it an advantage. No one ever forgets his or her name. Two of the three girls have kept their birth surname throughout their adult lives.

What had been a tendency from the time Laurie was a toddler became intensified and intractable after the death of her Dad and little brother. By turns irascible and querulous or accommodating and acquiescent, yet often confrontational, her siblings and I found her unpredictable. Although we didn't have a name for it then, I believed it related to her menstrual cycle. She had all the most prevalent symptoms of this thing we now call PMS - (premenstrual syndrome): depression, hypersensitivity, low self-esteem, and irritability. I did my best to intervene, placate, and perhaps actually ended up enabling her moodiness. I suspect I had been doing this most of her life to a greater or lesser degree.

By 1973, Laurie was teaching creative dance for the Recreation Department, as well as performing in dance concerts put on by the high school and Dance Theatre Davis, directed by Jean Jackman. In the high school production of Brigadoon in her senior year, she danced the role of Maggie.

In the summer of 1974, she attended a dance workshop at the University of Utah with people who have made dancing their career. At first she had hoped to transfer there, but discovered she couldn't get into the dance department for another year, so instead decided to go to UCLA, and then later transferred to Berkeley after trying a summer course at Long Beach State.

Laurie continued to spend a lot of time with Dave Scott for the last couple of years of high school. Dave's dad, Verne Scott, built a water polo goal for our swimming pool. Dave came over often, in the evenings, to swim laps and shoot goals. We went to many of his swim meets and water polo games. Dave became a fixture at our house even after he went to college. He was most patient with Laurie's on-again, off-again moods. She must have hidden it fairly well at school, as she received the "most inspirational" award for swimming and gymnastics.

She hid a lot, as it turns out. "I had dreams and couldn't say anything to anyone about them. I didn't want to talk much to you because I was afraid of how much it would distress you. I couldn't cope with how much you hurt sometimes."

The students and subsequently the teacher's group chose Laurie in 1972 to be Davis' Girls' State Representative at Squaw Valley. In an interview with the newspaper, she said that the girls passed a woman's rights amendment, allowing women to choose Miss, Mrs. or Ms. on voter registration or legal documents. We thought it ironic that, of all possible positions, Laurie was appointed Fire Chief, as well as a legislative advocate on the committee for improved screening for hiring prison guards and medical personnel who came in direct contact with prisoners. She thrived on this experience. On her return, she was interviewed for newspaper articles and gave speeches to her sponsors.

I do believe these girls were ahead of their times – way ahead on some issues! This experience enhanced Laurie's self-esteem, if only temporarily.

The reproductive system of a young woman is extremely sensitive to changes in emotional and physical stress, as well as to caloric intake. Laurie may have been over-training during this period with dancing, gymnastics and swimming. Always something of a "grazer", it didn't seem unusual for her to eat lightly, often just taking a yogurt cup, a hunk of cheese, and a piece of fruit in her backpack to eat between activities - thoughts about nutrition low on her list of priorities.

This poem Laurie wrote to me about that time reveals her sensitivity to her own issues:

> *Mama,*
> *What should,*
> *could,*
> *What may I do?*
> *With my time, my energy,*
> *my life.*
> *Tapering tears follow*
> *my mind's design,*
> *weaving a cloth that's*
> *hard to shape*
> *and easily broken.*
> *-Laurie*

Dance was a good diversion for her – expressive - but she now says, "I didn't at that point express much of what was really going on under the surface. She later told me, "Yes, I was active, but I also kept trying to get my body to reflect how I felt inside – empty and sad. And I got positive feedback for being thin from my friends, who commented on my slim figure, usually with envy." She did lose weight, but because for dancers being slender is an advantage and the norm, it seemed desirable to her. She says now, "I didn't recognize and wouldn't have known the significance of having lost more than 10% of my body weight." It became apparent she was not eating enough to compensate for the amount of calories her body burned with all of her activity. Without my noticing it, Laurie at 5'6" went from a 113-pound active and healthy 9th grader to barely tipping the scale at 100 pounds by the end of her sophomore year. This weight loss alone could cause what they call 'athletic amenorrhea', but at the time our doctors were more inclined to think it was connected to what they called "grief reaction." It may well have been a combination of things. The weight loss and her diet, along with the emotional stress, certainly attributable to grief, as well as what we now know was PMS, left her vulnerable to developing a complete loss of menstrual cycle (amenorrhea) or at least irregular menses.

At first, Laurie's doctor took the 'wait and see' approach, but as the time drew near for her to leave for college, he cautioned me that a continuation of this problem could result in loss of bone density or even loss of reproductive capability. He first prescribed progesterone to try to stimulate the return of her menses. When by mid-July this had had no effect, he prescribed birth control pills in the hopes these hormones would regulate her menses and perhaps help with the emotional issues, as well.

We were hopeful, but within a few days after she began taking the prescription, she became even more emotional – mercurial and impetuous – veering from one mood to another, much worse than usual. The doctor advised me to discontinue the treatment. Knowing that we were leaving on vacation, he gave me a prescription for Valium, to be given in case the symptoms became worse during our upcoming planned family trip to Mexico.

Mexico Revisited

Part 1: Always Open House in Acapulco

In August of 1973, Laurie, Marci, family friend Tim Magill and I flew from Sacramento to Los Angeles, where we rendezvoused with Mark, who flew in from Seattle. He had spent the earlier part of the summer living with family and working on a dairy farm in Enumclaw, Washington, as well as visiting relatives in Seattle. Mexicana Airlines delivered us in Acapulco, where my friend, Maguis, and her two teenaged children, Marguerita and Guillermo, met us as we came out of Customs. We were stunned by the humidity as we deplaned.

We had been invited to stay in the Ballesteros's condominium 'apartment,' but were not prepared for its spaciousness or its luxury. Louvered sliding doors of bleached cedar enclosed a marble-floored living area. These doors could be opened to create a huge covered patio-like living-dining room. Guillermo's company built this twelve-story condominium on a prime piece of real estate – dead-center facing Acapulco Bay. Their penthouse apartment afforded a spectacular view with a swimming pool at a lovely 90 F. the ocean at about 85 F. I was so glad to have been able to bring the kids for a holiday. We needed this time away together - time to regroup and reconnect. I'm only sorry Valerie couldn't be with us. She was finishing up her course work at UC Davis, so that she could start law school in the fall.

Mark, Tim, Laurie, Marci, Guillermo (the son), and Marguerita (the daughter) bodysurfed for a very long time that first day. Maguis and I went for a walking 'tour' of the immaculate beach and then watched them from the pool area. A lovely day, renewing this very natural friendship within a stone's throw of the sound and smell of the sea, Maguis and I tried out a Yucatan 'hammock' of beautiful woven cotton, large enough for two. Maguis and I picked up our friendship as though we never missed a day of seeing each other - kindred souls.

Laurie tried her Spanish out on Guillermo, who said, "I will speak only Spanish, so that you will learn more," but that didn't last long. Guillermo and the Ballesteros children, except for Javier, the youngest, are fluent in English and French, as well as their native Spanish, as they each spent a year in the United States at boarding school and a year in France for the express purpose of learning to speak the languages. Javier's turn will come when he reaches the age of twelve.

Their cook prepared all of the food for the family, and there seemed always to be neighbor children coming and going in Acapulco. Dessert that first night was ground up pecans and carrots, blended until pureed with condensed milk, served with a simple cookie. Delicious!

At nine the next morning we all sat around the table for a breakfast of scrambled eggs with sausage and chili sauce, mangos, papaya, watermelon, cakes, cookies and a most delicious coffee – special for us, but their usual fare. I went with Maguis to the meat market later in the day, where we watched the butcher prepare two and a half kilos (five pounds) of beef, one and a half kilos (three pounds) of pork filet, and six dozen eggs; the bill was $22.50 U. S.

We stopped at a small shopping center, so that I could purchase a pair of tooled sandals, as well as some 'preventive medicine. Maguis had advised me on my last trip to take a prophylactic dose of a Mexican version of Kaopectate, which is not available in the U. S. Interestingly enough, she told me that when they visit the United States, they also experience gastrointestinal problems – different water, different microbes than what our systems are accustomed to, we presume. In any event, I suffered no ill effects during my last visit with the aid of this 'preventive medicine,'" so I decided it was worth taking it again.

As we relaxed with a Planters Punch after lunch, George, the owner of the eleventh floor, came to visit, bringing an assortment of field glasses to help Mark and Tim with their 'girl watching' on the beach. Tim says, "Mostly a bunch of Kansas City school teachers, with an occasional exception now and then." Motor boats pulled parasails in front of the apartment, near where some of the kids were bodysurfing.

After a swim and 'making talk' around the pool, the cook served a marvelous lunch at the usual time of 3 p.m. - huge shrimp broiled with a garlic, oil, and parsley sauce with rice, baked bananas, chicken with potatoes, and another iced blended dessert of mangos and condensed milk. "It is always open-house in Acapulco," Maguis noted as one young child from another floor came up as we were having our coffee in the hammock and said, "Gracias par almuerzo. Era delicioso."

Even with my limited Spanish, I could tell she was thanking the Senora for the delicious meal.

[Photo: Laurie and Margarita seated in chairs; Martha, Maguis and Laura standing - learning new songs around indoor swimming pool.]

While we relaxed in the hammocks, chatting and listening to music the younger generation played on their guitars, the 'monsoon' arrived; sheets of tropical rain poured down. Everyone scurried to close the louvered doors. In the bedrooms, the girls discovered water flooding onto the floor. Guillermo declared, "This was an engineer's mistake that hasn't yet been corrected. The drainage step that should have been next to the wall is outside under the glass balcony. "

Towels saved the day and nine-year-old Javier learned a new English word – "Hustle!"

We went to the Black Beard that night for our light meal – a lobster feast. Laurie and Marci tried 'La Bruha' (The Witch), a rum Planter's punch with almond extract, a piece of sugar cane with a crab apple on top for a swizzle stick. No one asked for I. D. here. Mark had a rum and Coca Cola drink called a 'Cuba.' He is tall and looks older than his fifteen years. "They served me a mimosa on the flight from Seattle to L. A., too," he offered, as I looked askance. For him at fifteen, looking older is a mixed blessing. He may get away with ordering an alcoholic beverage on the plane and in Acapulco, but people expect more of him, too.

The guitarist and singer at the restaurant, who sang mostly American songs, was, to put it charitably, not very good. Maguis said, "I do not like his singing."

His very next words were, "Why not?"

"Our table must be bugged," Maguis said, as she placed an ashtray over a knothole in the wooden table. When once more he responded appropriately to something that was said, he must have wondered why we all laughed. Maguis was embarrassed to discover the Black Beard does not take all Mexican credit cards, but between us, we had enough cash to cover dinner.

We arrived home to find about fourteen young people, playing a word game while seated around, on, and about the "tablaro," an 8x10 foot square table in the center of the living room, with a wraparound sectional sofa situated around two sides. As Maguis said, "Always open house in Acapulco!" This same group had played charades the night before with our clan, so these young friends were waiting for us to get back from dinner for another game. Our kids decided, however, that you need an entirely different programming for charades in Spanish because of sound-alikes. They also decided you need a different timetable in Mexico, too. We hadn't left for dinner until about nine, and now let the games begin – at a bit after 11 p.m.!

After the game was finished, they talked for a long time. Mark got into a political discussion with Luis, attempting to explain some of our recent economic problems, according to Mark, due to Nixon's sending grain to Russia.

The next morning, I awoke early and, upon unbolting the door, found it was still raining. I was surprised to find that after a high tide, the beaches are actually as dirty as ours; the main difference being that in Acapulco, if you get up early enough, you can see men from each building out picking up debris and sweeping the beaches clean.

Continuing our tour of Acapulco, Maguis took us to Fort San Diego, built in the 1600's to protect the harbor, and then to the Hotel Miramar where we watched the famed diver. The Bay of Acapulco has many peninsulas and small bays with no industry other than tourism. When I expressed my shock about the cardboard 'houses' of the poor people on the hillside, Maguis said, "Cleanliness of the beaches during the rainy season is a problem because the rain washes their 'dirt' down the hill. The government works slowly, but – it works!" It rained very hard that afternoon, and they called it a hurricane, but it was not nearly as severe as the ones we experienced in New Orleans.

Although I had seen panhandlers in the San Francisco Bay Area recently, I hadn't seen much homelessness before. I'd seen poor dwellings in New Orleans, but nothing like this – probably especially shocking with almost hurricane level rains coming down in sheets. Shocking, too, I think, because of the extreme contrast between the affluence of those living in luxurious high-rise condominiums with swimming pools and cabanas, while barely a stone's throw away people lived in makeshift cardboard hovels, cold and perhaps hungry. I felt a little guilty as we headed off for yet another self-indulgent evening.

Maguis and I were invited with friends from another floor of the condominium to the casa of Senor Pani and Ed, his partner of some years. It was a gorgeous home atop a hill with what would have been a most spectacular view had Acapulco not still been in the throes of a torrential rainstorm. Maguis was pleased to see some water standing on their floors, too. She said it made her feel less embarrassed about their 'catastrophe.'

I enjoyed a tour of the house, which was elegantly decorated. A huge bouquet of blossoms of the "ixora", the beautiful red flowering shrub that can be seen everywhere in Acapulco, was the featured centerpiece of the entry to the spacious courtyard that was complete with a fountain and a keyhole of water from the swimming pool.

Spanish was the order of the day. I wished I had Marci's facility for just digging in and beginning or Laurie's fundamental knowledge; at least I might have understood "un poquito." As it was, Maguis interpreted for me occasionally; the rest of the time I gleaned the gist through picking up an occasional word I recognized.

After hors d'oeuvres of cheese melted on toast rounds, stuffed eggs, bacon wrapped fresh pineapple, and quiche, we went off to dinner at an Italian restaurant, where I enjoyed a 'safe' Caesar salad. Their appetizers are almost equivalent to our meals; they begin their evening meal at about the time I'm thinking about going to bed. My internal clock is being thrown way off kilter.

We were a bit worried about 'los ninos' because of the heavy rains and high water. They had gone with young Guillermo and the young people from the previous night's games to the Princess Hotel. We wondered how they had found passage on the streets. Maguis said, "There is really only one good road in Acapulco." They arrived home safely before us, and reported that they had a great time, dining and dancing.

I was concerned about Laurie, who seemed a bit on edge that afternoon. It is too bad that her self-image never seems to match how others perceive her; she looked so striking in the long yellow halter dress she wore that evening.

Part Two - No Hustle at Tequis

The next day we left for Taxco at 8:30 a.m. with young Guillermo driving. Mark had gone with Guillermo by plane the night

90

before back to Mexico City. The road was very narrow and curvy, but Guillermo proved to be a good driver. We shopped for several hours in Taxco. I bought several pieces of jewelry – a bracelet, earrings and a necklace designed by Los Costillo to match the bracelet Maguis sent me after my last visit. The necklace I bought last year for 500 pesos ($40) is now about $64. This time, I purchased a sterling serving piece for a present for the upcoming wedding of my niece Kathy.

We had lunch at the Hotel Victoria. Maguis and I finally came to an understanding about restaurant bills. We agreed that in the future, we would each pay for our own food, but Tim picked up this check. After lunch, which is traditionally about three, we drove to another of their homes, this one on Lake Tequisquetango, where Guillermo. Sr., Martha, Ilena, Laura and Javier were waiting for us, having driven from their home in the Pedregal. Friends from next door joined us for dinner. It's always Open House at Tequis, too. We found the hammocks most welcome after a long, but pleasant, day.

On Sunday, Lupé, the boat driver, took Tim, young Guillermo, Marguerita, and Maguis to Mass at the little church across the lake. From the boathouse deck, we could see them standing around the wall of the church; Guillermo said that he could even tell through the binoculars what part of the Mass they were celebrating.

A huge expanse of lawn, from the house, led down to the boathouse, which resembled a covered patio area with tables, hammocks, lounge chairs, and a barbecue. Water skiing, eating, backgammon, lounging in the 'hammocks' down at the boathouse area with many visitors coming and going by boat from around the lake were the order of the day. We were introduced to new-to-us hors d'oeuvres of jicama, a sliced root, sprinkled with lime juice, salt and chili, chilled and delicious – a refreshing snack, after which Lupe took us on a turn around the lake to look at the houses.

No "hustle" at Tequis, a lovely, peaceful place. We forget about all of the poor people, as we enjoy luxury.

Marci and Laurie worked with Laura and Ilena on gymnastics. Guillermo joined in. They learn quickly. Next they played a wild game of volleyball on an improvised net of a clothesline strung from a ladder to the balcony with towels draped over and more backgammon before bed. Guillermo and Laurie swam halfway across the lake. Never a quiet moment with this athletic gang! I enjoy the hammock and my book.

That last night at Tequis, we talked of the possibility of the Ballesteros family coming to Lake Tahoe with us for a skiing vacation. They've never skied. "We could rent a bigger house and entertain you in our custom – much less formal than Mexico, more like Lake Tequis!" I said.

Maguis protested, "It would be much trouble for you. No cook or household help as we have. We could not impose."

We argued that it would be no trouble at all - just different for them. We assured her, "We are used to casts of thousands. We live a bit more informally and everyone pitches in and helps with the cooking and clean-up." [And, in fact, the whole family never came to visit, but young Guillermo and a friend did come to Tahoe with us one weekend.]

Part 3 Tourists Again

Guillermo and young Marguerita went back to Mexico City in the early morning. Guillermo had to work. He said, "That is my only trouble." He has 35,000 employees working on a multitude of jobs currently under construction, including a road in Baja, California, a tunnel, three hotels, and a convention center. In fifteen days he was to start another hotel and 10,000 houses ($8,000 each) for the government.

Later, he took me on a tour of an area where he was building $2,000 houses for government employees. They are concrete block one room 8 x 8 houses with a bath and concrete floor. They share a common wall with their neighbors. These were not houses for just one person, either, but for families. This could be the answer to homelessness in the United States, but for the fact that no one would want them in their back yard. Housing purchases in Davis today start at nearly $200,000.

We drove to Mexico City after lunch. Mark, Tim, Marci and Laurie went with Guillermo and Marguerita to play squash while I went to the anthropological museum. The next day, Mark wasn't feeling well, but the rest of us went to Tepotzatlan, once a convent or monastery that is now a museum. The old church was very ornate. The new one in use is simpler, but painted in bright colors.

The next day we went to Teotihuocan pyramids. The construction is impressive. Some of the paintings are still visible - interesting designs in vivid colors. Rocks are of different colors, too.

We got home late to discover that a storm left the house with no electricity. Federico, a friend of the family who accompanied us to the pyramids, Guillermo, Marguerita, Laurie and Marci took turns

92

singing and playing the guitar in the dark for several hours. Guillermo taught them a French song: *Marche die Sacro et Vanzetti: Maintenant Nicolas et Bart, Vous dormez au fond de nos couers, Vous étiez tout seuls dans la mort, Mais par elle vous vaincrez.*

(I'll have to get out my French-English dictionary in order to translate. I'm afraid all of my French from college has vanished from my brain. Just an occasional word remains – maintenant = now, dormez = sleep, couers = heart, vous = you – oh, I think "vous étiez tout seuls dans la mort = You are all alone in death, but ..."

I have rarely thought about death and dying thus far on this trip.

The next day Maguis took us down to the colonial city – the Cathedral, the President's Office building where there are many beautiful murals. We visited the bank that used to be the Casa of the first Viceroy of Mexico. The same girl who guided Mickey and me through a few years before was again our guide. We went to the National Pawn Shop, where Mark bought a compass set. "An amazing collection of a lot of stuff – and at great prices," he proclaimed.

Guillermo took us to 'Del Lago' for dinner. As we ate our dinner, he said, "We could go to Lake Tequis again this weekend." We had planned to go to the Ballet Folklorico, however, on Sunday. "What do you think?" The prospect of going to Lake Tequisquetango again was too tempting. Without any hesitation, everyone agreed that to go to Lake Tequis for another wonderful weekend was preferable. Mark's plane was to leave early Saturday a.m., so Maguis said that she, Guillermo, and the younger children would drop him off on their way to the Lake. The rest of us packed our 'sundrisa' (smiles), swimsuits, suntan lotion, and a change of clothes, along with baskets of linens and the already prepared food, hopped in the car, and headed for Tequis.

Martha and her friend, Rosa, who had been there for a few days already, were surprised to see us. We arrived quite late, so Marci and Laurie told Rosa, the cook, and her daughter, "You may go to bed. We will prepare the dinner." They heated the soup we brought from 'home', put some cold ham on a plate, and heated some tortillas. Federico and Guillermo washed the dishes.

"Unheard of!" stated Martha. "They are just showing off for you." After dinner, we strolled out to the upper level of the boathouse for an evening filled with singing and guitar music in the 'hammockas.'

A note dated September 1, 1973 from Marci in my journal reads:

> *Para me mama…*
> *I love this vacation because of the people and everything. But I am especially enjoying it, because it is a family situation. It is relaxed. I am happy to be able to spend this time with you. Tequiero, Marci. Buenos nochés.*

The following day, more water-skiing for the younger set, rest, reading and conversation for the elders. Augustino and his sister came over from across the lake in the evening for an impromptu party. Laurie demonstrated her kind of dancing and then Martha and Laura (Augustino's sister) demonstrated Mexican dancing. There was much laughter, as each tried the others type of dance.

> *Laurie is at her most effervescent and exuberant when dancing. She glows during these times. I love to watch her graceful movements. I only wish she were always this way.*

Sunday we left fairly early in the afternoon because of anticipated traffic.

Part 4   Valle de Bravo and Back Again

Monday, Enrique drove us to Toluca to visit the Gomez family. Amalia prepared dinner for us before we left for a stay at their vacation home at Valle de Bravo. Their son Armando took Tim, Marci and Laurie to see the thirty-one horses at their ranch.

I visited with Alphonso and Amalia. They talked about Pancho (young Alphonso), who died in January as the result of an auto crash. They talked of him as the ideal son and compared Armando unfavorably to him. When Amalia showed me their family portrait, taken on their 25th wedding anniversary, she pointed out young Alphonso, "What a beautiful Niño!" I couldn't help saying, "Amalia, all of your children are beautiful – each in their own way - each beautiful."

I'm sad to hear them talk this way. It is difficult for me to be quiet. I want so much to urge them not to idealize Pancho. It must be difficult for the other children to know they suffer in comparison in their parent's eyes – especially when it is so unfair. I have tried so hard not to glorify either Keith or Glen. Have I been successful? I wonder.

Their driver, Antonio, drove us to Valle de Bravo, where we stayed for several days in their family vacation cottage. The trip was

94

beautiful, and Antonio and Laurie were able to communicate in Spanish. Antonio's eyes twinkled when I said, "He can understand every word we're saying, I'll bet."

Vicente, the caretaker, provided us with wood for a fire, which he lit when we got there; Alicia and Lucia offered us food from their cocina. We should have taken them up on it, but we were eager to get settled in for our week of living independently in a Mexican village cottage.

Tim and Laurie went to the village shopping for food as soon as we got settled. They found it an interesting experience. Our grocery list included lemons, cucumbers and onions at one place in the market, meat that was inexpensive but not marbled at another place, and Band-Aids (Curites) at the pharmacia.

Cooking in Mexico is a different experience. Our efforts were not especially memorable. I cooked the meat all afternoon to make a stew, and the meat was still exceptionally tough. "Now I know why Maguis went to a specialty butcher for her meat."

During the week before Antonio returned for us, we took many trips to the village for shopping in the market, as well as visiting the old church, which was very colorful, but simple.

Tired and irritable, that first night Laurie became irritated when Marci and Tim started a discussion. After dinner as we sat before the fire, for some reason she criticized Tim, unfairly I thought. I should have remembered how vulnerable and temperamental she had been for the past few days, but I grew impatient with her. She ran from the house and flew down the street into the dark village.

This hysterical episode is the worst I had ever experienced with Laurie. I wondered if there was something seriously wrong with her. Or could the effects of the pill still be lingering. I was anxious to get her home to see the doctor. And we, unfortunately, would be stuck in Valle de Bravo until Antonio came back for us four days from then. And then we would be in Mexico City another week before flying home to Davis – and a visit for Laurie with the doctor.

Back in Mexico City the next week, we had dinner at Del Lago with the Ballesteros family. Laurie seemed to be feeling better. She, Marci, and Martha enjoyed dancing with Tim and Guillermo to the live music. It was a delicious dinner with a lovely view and good music. Mariachi singers came and sang to us at the table.

We had lunch the next day at an old Hacienda near the Bazaar Sabado where we enjoyed shopping. Maguis was friendly and gracefully generous to the children who sold Chiclets, and to others sitting near the Bazaar, who appeared to be poor.

Before I left, I made a shadow portrait of each of the Ballesteros children, from which I later appliquéd quilt squares, alternated with embroidered squares of our memories of Mexico. I brought the finished quilt to them on a subsequent trip – a happy remembrance of our time with them.

Unresolved Grief

Upon returning to Davis, I immediately made an appointment for Laurie to see our family doctor. After a brain scan proved negative, the doctor suspected the cause of what might be described as a mild psychotic episode to be "the pill." Because of his uncertainty, however, he recommended psychotherapy in Los Angeles to assure she would have a successful year at college.

Laurie was accepted to the dance department at UCLA, but for some reason her housing arrangements went awry, so instead of being in a dorm, she lived for awhile as a boarder at a sorority. Probably not the best living situation, since it undoubtedly added to her feelings of isolation and loneliness. She soon met Jim Lutz, who was taking a dance class with her. Jim provided a support system for her in more than one way, as did frequent visits with her grandparents, who lived in Westminster, an hour away. Jim's car helped her get there.

When her friend Jim's plans to travel for several months after his June graduation caused what Laurie now says was an irrational reaction – an inability to tolerate again losing someone she cared about. Having him leave and be gone for several months reminded her of losing her Dad and Keith. She says, "Even though he left his car and his diamond ring with me, and there were ways we stayed connected, I shut down some part of the connection and reliance on him emotionally. Not on purpose, of course, but I just couldn't cope with another loss."

Some of Laurie's poems describe her state of mind at that time and for several years to come.

My mind,
masked by disguises conjured at some forgotten moments
to hide my naked fears and untidy imagination
now strains against the smothering folds of the garments
These cloaks which now cover me
allow the function but limit growth
hide wounds yet can't shield me from pain
and as they keep others from knowing my weakness
also keep me from knowing myself.
As I struggle to unfasten the aged apparel
the revealed fears seem almost friendly
the untidiness welcome in its exuberance
and I feel my spirit emerging and expanding
as the restricting fabric is loosened

           - Laurie

Laurie admits that her relationship with food was inconsistent. "My body sense, my sense of what was normal intake for me, my tendency to use exercise to help manage distress, and the tendency to feel "not hungry: all became formed in a significant sense during the time just after the fire when I couldn't really do anything to make myself feel okay."

By the end of her freshman year of college, she had gone back up to what would be a normal weight for her – about 115pounds. Her weight went down again when as a student at UC Berkeley, she danced in a dance piece set by a woman from the Cunningham Company. It was at that point that her sister Marci, with whom she shared an apartment, intervened, telling her that she was getting too thin. She saw a doctor at Student Health who agreed that her weight was too low and that she needed to get her weight back up. With Laurie, it wasn't what I consider true anorexia, e.g. deliberately denying herself food even when hungry in order to stay thin, requiring therapy to overcome the disorder. Laurie remembers responding positively to the doctor's warnings and immediately beginning to eat even when she wasn't hungry in order to gain weight.

While at Berkeley, Laurie met Craig de Recat, an actor and student at UC Berkeley. Like most aspiring actors, Craig waited tables, too. One night when he was our server at the Rusty Pelican in the Bay Area, he introduced us to the concept of "waiter magic," when appetizers and desserts appeared on our table without our ever having ordered them. After the semester ended, Craig headed for New York to seek his fortune and fame, leaving with us a cup from the Rusty Pelican, which I still use - a fond remembrance.

After graduating from Berkeley, Laurie decided to try dancing in New York City. Since Craig had gone before her, he already had an established living situation, which made Laurie's transition somewhat easier. She had, of course, planned to find a place of her own, but eventually I got the impression neither thought there was any great rush. I've got a picture of Craig in the loft, which shows the brick they discovered and uncovered as they continued to make a home for themselves.

This was the first Thanksgiving or Christmas Laurie had been away from home. She wrote that she and Craig and friends went up to Vermont for the fall colors. Laurie, an excellent correspondent, wrote often and expected letters in return. Laurie had many memorable experiences dancing in New York, even taking classes with Rudolf Nureyev.

By this time, Laurie wanted to be self-sufficient. She had graduated from college. She wanted to earn her own way. Always frugal, she had no trouble. She waited tables at Mumbles, a NYC bistro, earning enough in two or three shifts a week to support herself. She modeled Cappezio leotards for a national magazine, and performed with a few dance companies.

Craig waited tables, took acting and voice lessons, and performed in a soap opera and an off-Broadway show. By the time they decided to get married, Craig had come to the conclusion this was not a life style that was apt to support them. Perhaps his father had been right – although acting and dance were their passions, they were not practical. So they headed back to the West Coast, where Craig had been accepted into Loyola Law School and Laurie would return to UCLA to get a Masters degree in Dance Therapy. They were married in the backyard of our home on Elmwood Drive

In her mid-twenties, Laurie heard about this thing called PMS while watching the Phil Donahue Show. It was an 'aha!' moment for her. "Someone knows what's been happening to me. They've got a name for it – premenstrual syndrome. I'm going to call doctors until I find one who knows how to treat it." With the very first call to the Student Health Center the receptionist told her, "We have a doctor on our staff, who's doing research on that." That doctor prescribed a regimen of vitamins, called Optivite, that were low in calcium and high in magnesium. He also suggested a diet that included no caffeine and low sugar. She says, "It really helped." As a family, we noticed a drastic difference in her reactions, as well. We saw a more peaceful Laurie.

sensations with the power to rock my soul
gurgle up from some unexplored depths
hidden there by a terrified child
now encountered by the person the child has become
a fermenting mass just beyond awareness
bubbling sometimes into the present as an unexplained rage
or a flood of overwhelming sadness
sometimes terrifying, sometimes gentle
always prodding
till currents sweep me under water –
exploding – a streaming flood of sensation and emotion
and wash me onto shore
exhausted
conscious of the beauty trapped with the anger and pain
aware of the freedom to let go and explore
the option of becoming and growing,
until fears and confusion again block the flow
and the bubbling mass renews its insistent pressure
                                        -Laurie

Some time later, she decided, with the help of her therapist, that she was ready to "let go of Dad and Keith a little bit." She, Craig, and the therapist went up to a stream near Idyllwild, where she lit candles, talked, and said her goodbyes – a memorial service that she planned and presented. In her special way of solemnizing the occasion, she left little pieces of gold and flowers, and wrote this poem:

In Memoriam
Near a cathedral of granite and sky
where silence underscores all sounds
sparkling water rushing past
bestowing its cooling
calming spell
there I left roses and golden tears
among cedar trees and ferns
and pines
seasons and generations
pass through here in their time
and then pass on
      -Laurie

We had embraced Craig as one of the family, so it was with great sadness when their marriage ended. I continued to see Craig occasionally, having dinner with him when I was in L. A. for Market Week or a couple of times he has stopped by when he has had depositions to take in Sacramento.

Laurie finished her work at UCLA and then moved to Marin County and worked with the mentally ill in a residential treatment center there until shortly before her son Connor was born. Soon thereafter, she came and lived with us while she completed her studies to pass the examination for her Marriage and Family Counseling Certificate.

A family gathering while visiting my mother and step-father in Southern California: front row: Jack Adams, Ed, Craig holding Sean Henry; Laurie holding Lisa Henry; Marci, Rick Hagan; Back row: Mike Henry, Me, Valerie, Mark, and my mother, Bea Adams.

For a 1974 English assignment, Mark wrote...

For a 1974 English assignment to tell something about someone without writing about them, Mark wrote:

Her desk is beautiful. It's a secretary of cherrywood. Bookshelves rise above the drawers and cubbyholes where the secrets of the universe lie. The writing surface is cluttered with pictures, papers, bills, and books. Looking through the piles of miscellany one could find pens, glue, measuring tape, dried flowers, invitations to art shows, and invitations to parties. Material for books to be written and classes to be taught lie waiting for their time to be. All of this can be hidden from view by closing the front, the only way I have ever seen it cleaned.

Above the wonderful clutter are scads of little drawers and niches. Some tiny doors cover tiny spaces where tiny miracles are hidden until brought out to fascinate the eyes and fingers of a lucky child.

The book shelves hold miracles for older children. Trips in balloons, horses running, summer times and summer days are on the first shelf. The second has lives of loves, romance, intrigue, and mystery. On the third shelf are the secrets to finding the life to lead, to finding Madagascar, to finding right, acute and obtuse angles, and to finding the name of a bone in your little toe. On the top shelves are the questions, the ones you must try to answer when you are no longer a child. Questions like "Why did Romeo and Juliet die?"

Amidst the books on the shelves are treasures, things to look at and enjoy, like a picture of four little kids trying to milk an extremely patient cow. There is also a glass vase with deep facets in its curves. Also there is a wooden sculpture of a mother and her babe, something to look at and ponder.

It's my mothers' desk. It holds many things. It holds wonder, and it holds knowledge.

-Mark Snodgrass
1974

♠

Two years after Laurie went to Girls' State, Mark was nominated by the students and subsequently chosen by the teachers to represent Davis at Boys' State. There, the boys elected him Supreme Court Justice. He says, "I even got to share the podium with Governor Ronald Reagan." Interestingly, he tells me now that he felt much more accepted at Boys' State than he did at Davis High School; it was a very encouraging experience. He was nominated as First Alternate to Boys' Nation, and for some reason thought the reason he didn't get to go had something to do with his being a Unitarian. This impression corresponded with Laurie's that Girls' State wasn't entirely non-denominational, as it had been touted; they were required to say The Lord's Prayer. When she asked about it, she was told, "Everyone says The Lord's Prayer." She remembers the counselor being disbelieving when Laurie countered with, "Even Buddhists and Taoists?"

Mark sang with the Madrigal Choir and Jazz Choir under the direction of Dick Brunelle all through his high school years – he seemed to enjoy both, everything except wearing the tights as part of his Madrigal costume when they visited other schools. It wasn't so bad at Davis High – they were used to seeing them, but boys at other schools looked askance and made fun of them.

At the time, I would have said, "he enjoyed," but now I say "he seemed to enjoy," because on the outside, Mark seemed to have it all together – affectionate, outgoing, and well rounded. But on the inside ...maybe one never can be sure with a teenager.

Mark continued his interest in photography and stage lighting. He played on the water polo and tennis teams. Like Laurie though, part of his persona was a mask he wore, hiding his true feelings much of the time.

Each summer during his high school years he spent some time with his uncle; intuitively, I knew it important that he have that connection with the extended family and especially with his Dad's younger brother, a positive male role model.

It was in his first years at college that Mark experienced what we came to believe was a delayed grief reaction or post-traumatic stress syndrome – depression, sleeplessness and anxiety. I came to understand, during my work with Bereavement Outreach, that unlike adults, bereaved children do not experience continual and intense emotional and behavioral reactions. They may seem to show grief occasionally, but usually it's only brief and then they go back to their normal activities, sometimes acting out in inappropriate ways. In truth, however, a child's grief usually lasts longer than that of an adult – longer because a child's ability to experience intense emotion is limited, in time and intensity.

Grief comes and goes – ebbs and flows, like waves in the ocean: sometimes stormy, sometimes calm. Just as with adults, children first feel shock and denial, mixed with confusion and painful feelings. It can be a very confusing time for a child. It may take a long time for true healing to take place.

In both Laurie and Mark's cases, they didn't show their feelings as openly as the older girls and I did. They both threw themselves into activities, putting off what would inevitably one day have to be addressed. I believe their minds protected them from what was too sad and powerful for them to handle in their early teen years.

The Promise

In the fall of 1975, a man I'd met at one of the Sierra Club bridge gatherings and had been dating off and on for a few months, got a new job and moved to Georgia. He asked me to marry him, but honestly, I knew deep down that this was an uneven relationship. We had little in common. I love the theatre, ballet, classical music, the City; he liked country music, line dancing, and wanted to buy a farm. His sister and I, however, shared many of the same interests. Tired of being single and hating the dating scene, however, I let his invitation tempt me. I decided to visit him in Athens, Georgia. We had a great time – no line dancing! He showered me with attention; we toured Savannah, Atlanta, and even went to Hilton Head, S. C. I began to consider his proposal. I thought that perhaps I would open a Centering in Athens, and keep the one in Davis, traveling back and forth occasionally. I already had a possible manager for the Davis store – Jacquie, a woman who once was engaged to my friend, Ed, as a matter of fact.

By now, you must know that my entrepreneurial spirit gets aroused at the thought of a start-up of anything. This sounded like fun.

I wrote to Ed, who planned to pick me up at the airport on my return, and told him that I was considering getting married and moving to Georgia. I guess he should write the next part, but the way I recall it that gave us both pause! We both valued our friendship more perhaps than we had realized, when it was right there, always available.

Ed seemed to be grieving by the time I returned He suggested that we should think further about our relationship.

Relationship? What? More than a friendship?

As soon as I realized there was a chance that Ed and I might find our way to a serious relationship, I broke off the 'engagement,' as gently as I could. By this time, I knew I'd loved Ed all along. I just denied my feelings because of something over which I had no control, our age difference, an age difference that would never have been a consideration had it been the other way around - him ten years older than I.

From Ed's perspective, I think "a relationship" other than friendship had probably never crossed his mind either, until he got the news I might be leaving Davis.

We began to do more things together as a family might. One Sunday, Laurie, Marci, Ed, and his daughter Shelley, and I went hiking and picnicking on Mt. Tamalpais. Not surprisingly, Ed seemed to be getting cold feet about the thought of joining this family, or perhaps more to the point, marrying this woman, who seemed a bit threatening. The indomitable spirit, while admirable, seemed to leave him wondering if this was going to work. I had a few doubts myself, wondering how it would be when he was 60 and I was 70. Well, today I know, although we passed those ages ten years ago. While I currently am unable to do much walking, and find getting some places challenging, I encourage him to do all of the activities for which he is able – backpacking, ushering, flying, and together we enjoy theatre, ballet, and our time at home together. I remember thinking then though, perhaps rationalizing: We should just enjoy however many days we have - together one at a time. Nothing is certain in this life, as I'd learned, the hard way.

Ed and I were married on July 4, 1976, on the balcony of his mother's Alta Laguna Blvd. (Top of the World) home in Laguna Beach, California, surrounded by family – his and mine.

Newly graduated Mark would be able to go off to college and not have to worry about his mother being alone.

Today, when people say to Ed, "You aren't old enough to have a great grandchild twelve years old," he makes his usual jocular rejoinder: "I promised I'd never tell I married an older woman with children."

Docunt volentem fata, nolentem trahunt, carpe diem, quam minimum credula postero. (Loosely translated…Fate leads the willing, but drags along the unwilling one; seize the day, trust as little as possible in tomorrow.)-Seneca

A Legacy of Love

While at the University of Oregon on a competitive pre-med track, Mark experienced depression and anxiety attacks. The next year he transferred to UC San Diego, where he worked out with their crew – more *activity*. He rowed starboard stroke on the Lightweight Eight and Four. He was quite proud to have rowed stroke on the first UCSD boat to beat out UCLA in competition.

At one point when he experienced an intensification of depression and anxiety, Ed and I drove down to San Diego and brought him and his belongings back to Davis. For awhile he spent endless hours in his room, going out only to visit the therapist we found for him; he slept, ate, slept some more, and resisted socializing with anyone.

It wasn't until 1980 that what we now call Post Traumatic Stress Syndrome (PTSD) became a diagnostic category - a type of anxiety disorder that's triggered by a traumatic event. You can develop post-traumatic stress disorder when you experience or witness an event that causes intense fear, helplessness or horror. All of those of our family present in those early morning hours of January 1, 1971 experienced all of those. Little at that time was known about brain chemistry and the physiological changes that are precipitated by such dramatic and horrific events. Teenagers under normal circumstances experience brain chemistry and physiological changes. Mark, Laurie, Valerie and I experienced normal grieving, of course, but had the additional burden of what we now know is PTSD. For many children, PTSD symptoms go away on their own after a few months. Yet some children show symptoms for years if they do not get treatment. In 1971, we didn't know about it, so Mark and Laurie fell into that category.

Recognizing that I had somehow been negligent in understanding the depth of Mark's grief and what we now know was PTSD, my guilt at times became overwhelming. Don't we parents always feel responsibility for the well-being of our children? I became overcome with a sense of powerlessness - with an inability to make things better for Mark.

Ed and I saw a therapist, which helped me finally to come to believe that since I had been dealing with my own very intense personal grief at the time, I had probably done all I was capable of doing – my best - during the months and, indeed, years after Glen and Keith's deaths. Beating myself up wasn't going to be productive.

The most important thing to remember is that the past cannot be changed. All you can do is work through how you feel about those facts and move forward.

We eventually encouraged Mark to move into an apartment with a roommate, thinking that perhaps we had been enabling his reclusive behavior by allowing him to live at home in self-imposed isolation.

With the encouragement of his therapist, he eventually enrolled in some classes at UC Davis. He joined the Early Music Ensemble, which was invited by the Church of England to sing at Winchester Cathedral on the Fourth of July during the celebration of its 900th anniversary. They got to perform in London and then spent some time at Oxford rehearsing with the St. Mary's University Choir.

"That was really a spectacular experience," he wrote me recently. "We stayed in St. Mary's dorms, wonderful rooms, probably five hundred years old. We ate in the student dining room. You know – fifty-foot ceilings, huge portraits of long dead people, pewter

110

tableware and mugs. I remember getting wonderful fried kippers instead of bacon for breakfast. But I suppose what was most unique at the time was that here was a student dining room with sit-down table service. A far cry from the American steam table cafeteria experience.

"Performing at Winchester was exciting. A very fine musical space. And after the concert, we got in trouble for celebrating the Fourth of July. After we closed the Pub, one of the choir members whipped out the 'fireworks.' The local constabulary was not amused by a contingent of tipsy colonials reenacting the siege of Yorktown."

After singing in England, he hitchhiked through France, Switzerland and Italy, did some climbing, and hung out in tiny Alpine village taverns, drinking red wine with an international crowd of skiers, climbers, and old men.

When he returned to the States, he went to Seattle to spend time with his dad's brother, Dale Snodgrass. He says, "I remember walking up and down the streets of Seattle's warehouse district talking to businesspeople, leaving flyers, and generally pushing pencils" for Dale, who owned an office supply company. Probably more importantly, after going through a bleak squall, he had found an anchor. It is more than literary artifice to use nautical terminology when speaking of Dale and Mark's relationship.

Every summer for years Mark has spent a couple of weeks out on Dale's boat up in the San Juan's – fishing, eating mounds of crab, and talking man-to-man. "In fact," Dale says, "For several years, I counted on Mark to keep the engine running."

He never liked to back-flush our swimming pool when he was sixteen or mow the lawn. Who knew the kid would grow up to be mechanical?

Working for Dale is where he began working with computers in earnest – and he says, "That's when I really began to heal." He flew to Sacramento when the University dedicated a family waiting room at UC. Davis Medical Center Burn Unit to honor Glen and the contribution he made to the medical school. He toured the burn unit, and I believe that may also have been a turning point for him – a bit of accommodation - not closure - at twenty-one that he had not been able to do at the age of thirteen. Mark and Laurie both used activities to fill "the emptiness" until they could deal with it later.

Closure is not a word I use lightly – or ever – with the fire that caused the sudden death of a parent and sibling such as we

111

experienced. As Valerie wrote me recently after reading a draft of the book, "It's an amazing journey you've made over the last forty years – that we've all made. I think what surprises me is that it's never really over. It's not something you ever 'recover' from. We all are who we are – richer for our lives with Dad and Keith and different as a result of their deaths. Not bad-different, but clearly different than if we hadn't had to work so hard to find the good."

Mark set up a computer system for his uncle's business and then for others up and down the Coast. He enrolled at the University of Washington, where he graduated magna *cum laude* with a degree in business in 1984. He and Pam, whom he had met while living in that apartment complex three years earlier when he was a student at UC Davis, were married that August in the Tulip Garden of San Francisco's Golden Gate Park with a reception at the Cliff House.

Mark is very much like his dad was, in that he takes great pride in his family. He also has that deliberate way of speaking and with that same resonance. I feel confident that there's a bit of Devil's Advocate in him, too. He delights in a good discussion.

The hidden gift behind bereavement for Mark, Laurie – in fact, for all of our family, is that so much was taken away from us that we've become grateful for what we have. It is worth noting, that every member of our family has gone - in one form or another - into a helping profession: Valerie, a middle school math teacher for many years, now teaches teachers to teach math at UC Irvine. Marci, a well-respected family practice/OB doctor, even makes house calls. Laurie, a therapist, is known for her work with adolescents and now supervises therapists of clients with eating disorders. Mark owns a software company and writes software for financial planners to help their clients plan for college for their children, for retirement, or for the unexpected loss. I still tutor young children, who have not learned to read in a traditional classroom setting, as well as writing skills to older children and young adults.

As I learned years ago, when you least feel like getting out of bed in the morning, it helps to remove the pain and sorrow if you do something for someone else. We can take some small comfort in this legacy of love that Glen and Keith left behind - this good the ill wind did blow.

The Blue Shutter Inn

Shortly after we were married, Ed and I returned from a vacation in Ashland, Oregon, still talking about the plays we'd seen, the scrumptious dinners we'd had at Chateaulin, and the long walks in beautiful Lithia Park. My children, who had been going to Ashland nearly every summer since 1960, said, almost in unison, "We want to go next year."

Ed immediately placed an ad in the Ashland newspaper: "Vacation house wanted for large family." At that time we were a family of eight, including one young grandchild.

We didn't know then what a large family was!

Within days, we had a response: "I've got a pioneer house just a few blocks from the theater that I would be willing to rent to you. Do you think $25 a night would be too much?" The owner said she'd welcome having someone housesit while she went to visit her children in Seattle. She cautioned, however, that the little one would have to wear shoes because of the wood floors, so we didn't expect too much, but it would be a roof over our heads and a bathroom and a half. That was all that we would need.

I'll never forget the day Ed and I drove up to the house a day ahead of the others. "123 Church Street? This can't be it," I muttered, as I looked first at Doleen's letter and the map she'd sent us, and then again at the numbers on the beautiful white two-story house with blue shutters.

"This is a far cry from what I would call a primitive pioneer house," I said. Inside, those 'splintery' wooden floors were beautiful Swedish-finish hardwood. The furnishings may have been a bit sparse, but this was far from the picture we got in our minds when we had talked with the owner some months earlier.

This was to be the first of several years we rented the house, twice a year, for family vacations. After several years, Doleen told us, "Sadly, this will be the last time you'll be able to rent the house. I'm going to have to sell it. I just can't keep it up anymore. The garden is too much for me. And it needs painting, a new roof. I just can't afford to keep it."

Without so much as a second thought, nor a quibble about the purchase price, we agreed we should buy it for our family. It felt like home by now. An attorney in Ashland helped us with the sale. Doleen continued to live in the house for two years, as we wall-papered, painted, and decorated and furnished it to make it our own.

Over the years this turn-of-the century home had been "remuddled", the most egregious to my eyes a sliding glass door to the backyard from the dining area of the large living room. This was one of our first changes as it looked just too modern. We installed a mullioned atrium door.

On one of her vacations, Marci created a blue iris stained glass window to replace a rather ugly mustardy-yellow plastic one beside the front door. Another time, she made one for the landing of the stairs. It can be seen at night as one walks down Church Street from Scenic Drive.

Ed and our son-in-law Mike put in drip irrigation for the new cutting garden we decided upon, and for the rose garden in the front yard. Our Ashland friends Mara and Nikos Mikalis recommended a friend of theirs to help with our gardening.

Joanie Nissenberg, a Master Gardener, took over the landscaping and has acted as caretaker of the house ever since, helping us with many of the tasks necessary to get repairs made. For instance, when the pipes burst one winter, because the power went out all over Ashland, she was the one who called us and helped to make arrangements to get new flooring installed. When Joanie decides she no longer wants to take care of our garden, I fear we'll have to sell the house. She's one of a kind!

Joanie paid special attention to the English cutting garden the year Marci and Peter asked to be married in the Ashland back yard. It formed the perfect backdrop, as the minister pronounced them man and wife under the big old black walnut tree.

We regret to say the ancient walnut tree became unsafe and had to be removed. Because of extensive building in the hills a few years ago, deer invaded our property, so the cutting garden has been replaced with more deer resistant plants. The October red maple tree, we planted near the big stump of the black walnut, which started out as a staked-up reedy stick, is now as tall as the house; it has grown up with the grandchildren. In the front yard, an interesting bamboo fence and a rosemary hedge protect the rose garden from the picturesque, yet unwelcome, deer.

Ashland has been a perfect vacation spot for all of our family – sometimes a rendezvous spot when Mark and his family drive down from Corvallis, as the rest of us come up from Davis and all points south.

Our family has grown up – and grown up well.

Valerie, married with two adult children and one grandchild, finished her Ed.D., and teaches teachers to teach Math at U.C. Irvine, for the Irvine Unified School District, as well as others in Southern California.

Marci, after several years as Director of Intramural Sports at Cal Poly San Luis Obispo, went to Medical School at Michigan State University. When she, her husband Peter and their two children planned to come back to Davis for her residency at U.C. Davis Medical Center, we couldn't find a suitable home for them in their price range, so we moved into a small duplex while they rented our Elmwood house. Later when Marci signed on to practice with a U. C. Davis Medical group – family practice and obstetrics – they bought the

116

home, as by this time a single story home seemed most practical for Ed and me.

Laurie gave up her dancing career and studied to get her Marriage, Family, Children Counselor (MFCC) certificate. She and her husband, Jim Wheeler, also live in Davis, where, as a therapist at an eating disorder clinic, she now works with families, children and adolescents, as well as supervising other therapists.

Mark graduated from the University of Washington in business, after overcoming the delayed-grief reaction he experienced during his first few years of college. To be honest, it takes time to overcome a delayed-grief reaction. It is akin to PTSD (Post Traumatic Syndrome). Things still crop up from time to time for all of us, I believe, that take us back. It's that ebb and flow thing I mentioned earlier. Married and with three daughters, two off to college and one now working at a Kipp School in Denver with Teach for America, he now writes financial planning software and is a co-owner and president of Money Tree, Inc. Following in Mark's tracks, one nephew played water polo at Davis High School, and his nephew and niece, Connor and Chelsea, both graduates of Davis High School, sang with the award-winning Madrigal choir. Ed and I travelled with the choir to Llangollen, Wales to hear them in an Eistedfodd in which they won Best Chamber Choir and competed for Best Choir in the World. Mark, Connor and Chelsea joined other returning Madrigals in a 40th reunion concert at Mondavi Jackson Hall, honoring Dick Brunelle, who founded the Madrigal Choirs at Davis Senior High.

In Sickness and in Health – 35 Years! Celebrate!

One usually thinks of going out for a romantic dinner to celebrate one's anniversary, but not Joan and Ed Callaway. We start our celebration by setting up our folding chairs in front of Munchie's to get a good seat for the parade; the beginning of all-day festivities in Ashland, Oregon, which we choose to believe are especially in our honor. For thirty-four years we have been going to Ashland, many times rendezvousing with our whole family to celebrate the anniversary of the day we gathered on the balcony of Florence Callaway's Top of the World home in Laguna Beach, overlooking the ocean on that sunny 4th of July in 1976.

The jets fly overhead to announce the beginning of the parade. Bands play as everything from marching won-tons and deck-chair Yuppies to little ballerinas pass by. An antique fire truck, full of Dixieland musicians, manages to finish the parade route and race around to re-enter and repeat their performance at least three times.

We especially like to sit in front of Munchies, as it is just a couple of blocks from our vacation home, but I must confess it's probably also because it's only steps away from lattés and cinnamon rolls for breakfast. It's also on the direct route to the bandstand through what we affectionately call 'pork-out ridge' - the street behind Lithia Park that is closed off on this special day. Artists and non-profits set up hundreds of food and arts-and-crafts booths, providing sustenance and temptation for the parade-goers on their way to and from the bandstand up the hill.

One of the actors from the Ashland Shakespearean Festival reads the Declaration of Independence. A high school student presents the winning patriotic essay of the year, and the mayor introduces visiting gaily-costumed guests from Ashland's Sister City in Mexico. And then, the piéce de resistance, the Ashland Community Band presents a full afternoon of toe-tapping John Phillip Sousa marches. People-watching provides even more entertainment, as friends and neighbors greet each other on the blanket and chair-covered hillside above the bandstand.

It's a thrill when the conductor of the band invites veterans from each of the armed services to stand as the band plays their hymn.

We keep waiting for him to announce our anniversary, but each year he forgets. Never mind.

We know the fireworks are yet to come. Most often now, though, our day has been so full that by dark we are ready to call it a day and let the younger generation do the ooh-ing and aah-ing for us. We are far too stuffed from the traditional sausage sandwich and the other sumptuous delights we weren't able to resist as we passed by 'Pork Out Ridge' on our way home. Who could even think of going out to a romantic dinner after such a day? Our senses are sated in every way.

Ed and me at the Ashland City Band concert, admiring Connor's painted face –July 4, 1992.

'...One for the Gipper"

From a June, 2004 journal entry

My interest in politics began with the Jerome Waldie political campaign back in 1974. As one of Nixon's most outspoken critics, Waldie had been one of the first members of the House Judiciary Committee to call for impeachment, after the firing in October 1973 of Watergate special prosecutor Archibald Cox, who had angered Nixon by demanding the release of crucial White House tapes. My interest in politics never faltered from then on.

The President Ronald Reagan that I remember was affable, familiar, and always ready with a quip. He was not, however, the paragon his mourners would have us believe him to be. While I sympathize with Nancy Reagan and the rest of his family for the debilitating Alzheimer's disease he and they have long endured, many of his policies I found a little like Robin Hood gone amok – taking from the poor and giving to the rich.

He graduated from Eureka College, a small Christian school near Peoria, Illinois, not far from his family's home. This exposure undoubtedly led him to some of his conservative views.

My first memories of him, of course, were from the movies and later as host of TV's General Electric Theatre. He played in several unremarkable and unmemorable movies, but one I remember is Kings Row in which he played a small town playboy whose legs were amputated by a careless surgeon. He got his nickname from the role of Knute Rockne, All American, the Notre Dame football hero, George "The Gipper" Gipp, in which he delivered the immortal line, "Win one for the Gipper."

It was his five-year term as President of the Screen Actors' Guild that started his political career. Very concerned about communism in the United States, he willingly testified before the

House Un-American Activities Committee, leading to the blacklisting of several actors. He later became an FBI informant.

I found few of his policies palatable. His indifference to the pleas for help in the blooming AIDS crisis delayed the slowing of this plague. He opposed affirmative action and racial quotas at a time they were necessary for African Americans to progress in academics and employment. He sought a tax credit for segregated Bob Jones University, which infuriated the black population. When the air traffic controllers went out on strike, Reagan interfered with the union and fired them all, as I recall, which caused chaos until new controllers were trained and in place. As governor, he proposed more tax increases than any governor before or since. What I recall most favorably about President Reagan was that when confronted with evidence that his tax cuts were fiscally irresponsible, he was not ashamed to change course. Or his mind. He signed the California Therapeutic Abortion Act, but then later said that he regretted having signed it. He stayed away from that issue after that as much as possible.

I did not and do not approve of Reagan's economic policies, which left the nation with trillions of dollars of debt, nor some of the foreign policy hanky-panky, notably the Iran-Contra scandal, which ultimately led us into the current Iraq debacle. Still, he did, however, forge relationships with Mikhail Gorbachev that eventually led to the tearing down of the Berlin Wall and the critical push that led to the end of the Cold War and the Soviet Union. It should also be noted that President Reagan at one time supported Osama bin Laden.

It is interesting how our one-time friends can turn out to become our worst enemies. And how short our memories are – with or without Alzheimer's disease.

According to an Associated Press article in the Sacramento Bee at the time of his death, perhaps "President Reagan's sweetest legacy is his love of Jelly Belly's." The company began shipping the miniature jelly-beans to Governor Reagan when he decided to quit smoking back in 1967. Reaganomics really worked for the Fairfield Jelly Belly Company as it has grown to 670 employees, shipping 13 billion jelly beans a year!

The body's hardly even cold and this afternoon, as the casket was making its way down Connecticut Avenue, my e-mail brought me an offer for a "rare two-disk box DVD set" of "Ronald Reagan: The Great Communicator." And so it begins. First we canonize him and now we're going to capitalize on his memory.

Some of the hardest hit under the Reagan administration fiscal policies were Medicaid, Aid for Dependent Children, and food stamps – in other words, the poor. His Agriculture Department wanted to define ketchup and relish as vegetables for the school lunch program!

As Governor of California, he was responsible for downgrading the state hospital system in the early 1970's with the closure of three state mental hospitals. It was believed that the new psychotropic drugs would make hospitals obsolete. The mental health realignment shifted the responsibility for mental health programming from the State to the counties of California. However, the promise of adequate state monies followed for only a time, but due to recessions and reduced tax revenues, the promise had not been kept.

The most visible effect of hospital closures and reduced funding to the Counties was the increasingly large number of mentally ill who could be found wandering the streets, parks and malls, sleeping under bridges, in doorways, in shelters, or if they were very lucky, in cheap motels.

A Place to Belong

In the mid-70's, as President of the Yolo County Mental Health Association, I attended the annual meeting of the Mental Health Association of California in Los Angeles, where I received an award for my work with Bereavement Outreach. Recognition is appreciated, but, as far as I was concerned, meeting the many parents of the mentally ill, as well as Murray Levine, who was Executive Director of the Marin Residential Treatment Center and the Great Crepe, a restaurant vocational program, highlighted the meeting.

Conversations with Murray that day inspired me to go a few weeks later to visit him in San Rafael with Pat Williams of Davis, activist parent of two mentally ill sons. We visited the Farmhouse and had lunch at The Great Crepe, largely staffed and operated by client cooks and waiters under the direction of staff.

For more than a hundred years, California provided care for the mentally ill in eleven state hospitals, which essentially functioned as warehouses, with patients being admitted for unspecified periods of time and receiving little or no treatment. In the 1950's, the advent of psychotropic drugs led to the de-institutionalization movement that radically changed the treatment of the mentally ill in California. With the passage of the Short-Doyle Act, the large state hospitals were replaced with county-operated, local mental health systems. Thousands of mentally ill persons were transferred to communities that lacked support services to adequately meet their needs.

Programs such as the Marin county model seemed an ideal solution to a growing problem. I came back to Davis and immediately wrote a grant proposal for a vocational program for Yolo County. The proposal, with the approval of the County Mental Health Director, Captane Thomson, I submitted to the California Department of Vocational Rehabilitation. It unfortunately was rejected. It later; however, became the foundation of the vocational component of a proposal submitted by Yolo County Mental Health in response to AB 3052, the legislation known as the Bates Bill.

My vision at that time was for a restaurant or a bakery or a combination of the two. What actually evolved was a gardening and office cleaning service, known as Headway.

While the Yolo Mental Health Director, Dr. Captane Thomson, signed off on the community-based proposal, I believe he never truly expected this small rural county would be the recipient of enough money to make a significant difference. To everyone's surprise, Yolo County was awarded enough to fund the entire circle of service proposal – or so we had thought.

Our struggles with the County had just begun. [Caveat: Please remember what I wrote in the Preface: "Whatever I write are only my truths, my perceptions," and that others may not recall events and exchanges in the same way. I think that is often the outcome from an adversarial situation.]

We promoted the idea of a social rehabilitation model, whereas it seemed that Dr. Thomson believed in the medical model, which involved giving clients medication and monitoring them occasionally with brief appointments, believing that would be 'as good as it gets.' This wide divergence in philosophy caused a clash that would be on-going for the foreseeable future.

Our proposal included a mental health practitioner as an integral part of the residential treatment circle of services. The County, however, envisioned that as a way of gaining another psychiatrist on their staff. Cap said, "You will not be doing therapy. You won't need a therapist. The County will do whatever therapy is done, so we'll need another psychiatrist on our staff." And with that, from our perspective, they siphoned off a substantial portion of the funding and left the system with no immediate psychiatric supervisor directly responsible to YCCC's Executive Director and readily available to provide cohesiveness to our program.

In addition, the County claimed to need another large portion of the funding for overseeing the finances of the program. An accountant, Dan Frank, was immediately hired to monitor the finances of this embryonic non-profit. In fact, his main function seemed, at least to us, to be one of number crunching and impeding our progress with little cooperation or help. The perception of members of the Board of Directors: This same co-dependency, paternalistic relationship of "asking Dan," (more like pleading, with Dan, coaxing or manipulating) for funds we needed to make our programs function, continued for the duration of his employment.

Cap and I had been friends for many years. That friendship in some ways complicated the weekly and sometimes twice weekly meetings of the newly formed founding board of what came to be known as the Yolo Community Care Continuum or Y Triple C as it became known (http://y3c.org/). It sometimes took intervention of County Supervisor Betsy Marchand to mediate our heated discussions. More than once, I tried to convince Cap that this agency would one day be a feather in his cap, an innovative model treatment system of which he would be proud, if he would just let us go ahead and do it. He did seem to take pride in what we'd done when showing international visitors around the Farmhouse or the Socialization Centers, but to our chagrin, that pride did not carry over into the fiscal deliberations when budget time came around.

The power struggle continued for months...and, in fact, resumed on numerous occasions over the years between a series of Mental Health Directors, YCCC Executive Directors, and YCCC Board Presidents. I repeat – the relationship is much like that of an adult child who continues to be financially dependent on a parent. As long as that dependency remains, there are control issues. So it has been over the years with the contract relationship between the County and YCCC. At this writing, I'm not privy to their current relationship, but suspect that some things never change.

In retrospect, Bereavement Outreach was the first good the ill wind did blow. It led me to the Mental Health Association where I learned of the plight of the mentally ill and their parents. I view YCCC as the second good that ill wind did blow.

The following script I wrote and narrated for a YCCC slide show; a community education tool that we used for several years describes the program as it existed then.

> *A place to live. A place to work. A place to make and enjoy friends – friends who understand our possibilities as well as our limitations. One of our basic needs – a place to belong.*
>
> *A need that for generations was denied those with mental disorders. There was not that place to belong. There were not those friends who understood our limitations, much less possibilities! A place to live was often a cheap motel. A place to work? Not likely! Nor were there places to relearn social skills in a sheltered environment. And for a young person recovering from mental illness, a community – even the one he or she grew up in – could be a very frightening place.*

There were a few progressive communities providing residential treatment using what had become known as "the social rehabilitation model." These programs were so successful they attracted the attention of legislator Tom Bates, which led to legislation in California known as the "Bates Bill" and funding for a few pilot social rehabilitation programs. Through the efforts of a grass-roots movement, Yolo County's Mental Health Services was awarded a grant through the Bates Bill in 1979. They contracted with a local community-based non-profit, the Yolo Community Care Continuum, usually referred to as Y Triple C, to provide Bates funded programs - a circle of services designed to help adults, struggling with mental illness, to rejoin their communities in a supportive and structured environment. A system that would provide – at last – that place to belong.

All people need to feel capable, deserving of respect and status. We need caring; we need good nutrition, humane housing in a home-like environment. Y Triple C offers all of these with a social system of intervention – a continuum of care – and caring, with programs planned to develop coping strengths without furthering institutional dependency.

Safe Harbor Crisis House offers short-term intensive care in a structured home-like environment. Six beds – 24 hour care, offering both men and women a first step out of crisis – a safe place to land, an environment of friendliness and support. In this intensive care setting, clients are encouraged to regroup, look at options, return home, or move into an appropriately structured residential setting.

Perhaps the Farmhouse could be an alternative to long-term hospitalization – a home with a capacity of nine, staffed 24 hours a day, with educational and pre-vocational opportunities right there on the grounds. A wonderful place to live...open...lots of space...quiet... a garden...animals to care for.

Here we have an excellent example of a Community Residential Treatment system at work: Daryl moved from The Farmhouse after his 19-month stay, moved into his own apartment. He went to East Yolo House, one of two social centers that provide peer support, a network whereby our members provide each other with emotional, recreational, as well as practical support. Activities range from just hanging out to organized community meetings – member directed meetings. Decisions and plans are made at these meetings by members with the knowledge that only their energy and interest will make them happen - that they are responsible. This means that members know through experience that they have power and can, with their friends, change things.

Problem solving for most people involves talking with friends and relatives...a social network. A recent study found that people with mental illness, those with perhaps the most crucial need for such a network, have the fewest resources. YCCC expands their circle of friends.

Although a permanent place is important, each program takes pride in its outings. For each outing there is a long range plan, including perhaps a fundraiser, since most members live on very limited budgets. While they are making their plans, working on committees, having their fundraisers, the clients are learning new skills, assuming responsibility, and making new friends – with each other...with staff...and with people in the community.

East Yolo House, one of two social centers, serves 30-40 people a day, many of whom are homeless. Staff here and at the Dual Diagnosis Homeless Program assist on a regular basis in the daily trials of clients; finding places for them to live, providing meals or food baskets, transporting them to doctor appointments, or advocating and intervening for clients with social security, health and welfare departments, the justice system, etc. They are truly Jacks and Jills of all trades.

The Representative Payee Program is another service provided by YCCC to mental health clients who have been identified by the Social Security Administration as being unable to effectively meet their financial obligations. The goal of this program is to teach money management skills to participants who wish to achieve financial independence, as well as to monitor their expenditures.

It has been proven: that working clients become more independent, gain more self-confidence, require less intensive treatment and have lower reversion rate than non-working clients. Vocational programs such as Headway are essential parts of rehabilitation.

Traditional vocational rehabilitation programs measure success by how many files can be closed - how many people can be moved out of the program permanently. Success at YCCC is measured in terms of growth...in terms of quality of life...in terms of possibilities...in terms of capabilities no matter how large or small...in terms of growing to one's own potential;

living to the highest level of functioning, whatever that might be..

To some that may mean getting completely out of the system; to others it may mean always needing the support of the circle of friends at YCCC. That should be available without stigma…without shame…without question.

YCCC programs reduce the ranks of tomorrow's institutional dependents. It provides an answer to managed care in California's health care crisis. The community is enhanced not only for our members, but for all of us…by a new humanity, a network of friends, of mental health professionals and of families, as we will all work toward that common goal…a place for each of us to belong.

Note: Sadly, due to financial constraints, some parts of the program no longer exist. For instance, the socialization centers have been replaced with more independent or semi-independent living opportunities. An up-to-date look at the program with client videos can be seen at http://y3c.org/aboutus/

The YCCC Board of Directors established term limits for board members and officers, even before the public in their infinite wisdom voted term limits for our legislature. I still think it is a good idea to bring new blood into the agency, although it is beneficial to have some sense of continuity and history.

In order to be a part of the founding board of YCCC, I resigned from the Mental Health Association of Yolo County (MHAYC), where I had been President, believing it would be a conflict of interest to be a director of both YCCC and the non-profit watch-dog of the County on which the new agency would rely for its funding.

Eight years later, with my term at YCCC up, I had more time to devote to my business. While I continued to hear from various board members and staff from time to time over the next several years, I had nothing to do with the running of YCCC.

One day in the early 90's, however, I had a visit from a couple of staff members of YCCC, asking me if I wouldn't please consider coming to a Board Meeting that night to help mediate a conflict between the staff, some Board members, and the Executive Director. A crisis was in the offing! They felt that the Director's job was unfairly in jeopardy, and feared the possible outcome.

I attended the YCCC Board meeting, but was unable to accomplish much. A strong group had already coalesced and garnered support from enough of the board members to show lack of confidence in the ability of the Executive Director. The Board voted that night for one of the Program Directors to become Acting Director. The President that night asked if I would consider rejoining the board during this critical period. I agreed for a time limited and specific purpose: to help rebuild the board, which had by this time dwindled down to only a few members.

Surely I could find a few people to join the board of this valuable non-profit agency. The son of one of my best friends had just moved back to town with his family from New York where he'd been involved with the stock market. He hadn't been in town long enough to have been snapped up yet. I'll call him. And one of my customers, who worked in the California Legislative Analyst's Office, an accountant – she'd be a good prospect. And what about my neighbor across the street, who works with vocational rehabilitation at the University? I worked with her husband years ago at the University; he's superb at organizing and mediating. And, for sure I will call my friend Nancy Keltner from Mental Health Association days. We'll need her to do for YCCC what she did for MHAYC - publicity and fundraising. I'll put my persuasive hat on!

.[Photo: At the opening of The Farmhouse, First Executive Director, DickCahoon and Dr. Captane Thomson, Supervisor Twyla Thompson,, staff, and some of the founding board members, including Pat and Bill Williams, Rob Stone, and me behind the hay bale.]

A New Venture

On the business front, Janis Buckham Berry managed Centering so well that I was hardly needed anymore. She was an expert at buying earrings and greeting cards, which were the mainstay of the business, although I continued to bring in interesting gift items and now and then a few pieces of ethnic clothing from around the world.

Satisfied customers kept urging me to bring in more clothing. Kim McKnight, a new employee, who had previously worked at Pauline's, a women's clothing store, volunteered to help me learn how to approach the clothing market through the fashion industry shows in San Francisco and Los Angeles. Until that time, I had been doing my buying through the Gift Shows, primarily in San Francisco.

This opened up a whole new horizon for me. With my gift-jewelry store and my volunteer work, I had finally defined myself as something other than a bereaved widow and mother. Fate had led me in directions I had never dreamed.

Bob Warren, my landlord at 230 G Street, was just completing construction on a new building designed for retail and the First Northern Bank of Dixon. I rented one of the spaces along with a town-house apartment across the parking lot from where the new store would be located to house the 'back room' and office for the store.

Merry and I had named the art gallery/gift/jewelry store Centering, not only because of our interest in pottery, but because of its reference to the opposite of 'torn-to-pieces-hood.' I wanted a similar name for the clothing store, only something with a foreign sound to it; at the time, I planned to focus on ethnic clothing.

Coincidentally or perhaps serendipitously, I was reading a book about Whirling Dervishes, who in their whirling seek 'tariqa,' an old Persian word which translates as 'the way,' or something closely akin to 'centering.' Tariqa and Tariq are common Iranian names, meaning 'little girl star' or 'star.' I anglicized it by using a 'k' instead of the 'q', and hired a designer to create a foreign-looking rendition of the name for the logo of the new store. Marilyn and Charles Judson began constructing the new wooden signage for the front and back of the store.

Since I anticipated my new store would do for clothing what the first store did for gifts, this name seemed apropos. Centering! Stardom!

Delberta Hurley, who had helped me decorate my new house, again came to my rescue, helping me to design the interior furnishings and props for a women's clothing store.

We made trips to San Francisco in our search for some antiques, but eventually found everything we would need in Benicia, at Pier Group Antiques; they imported items suitable for store fixtures. An antique apothecary with ninety-nine drawers and innumerable cubbies of varying sizes would be perfect, although it would need some TLC. We refinished it, added white porcelain knobs, and replaced the white enameled tin numbers – and it was perfect. The antique English nursery rocking horse and pewter crib would add ambiance, as would the French birdcage I spray painted gold.

I'd been going to the San Francisco Gift Show for several years, but our first trip to the S. F. Apparel Market was an exciting, heady, exhausting, and somewhat frightening experience. That first market caused many a sleepless night. Would the merchandise come in all at once? Or would it come staggered as I hoped? Would the sweaters I ordered from one vendor come in to coincide with the arrival of the skirts and pants from another - or would a style be sold out and never arrive? Was I committing too much of my budget to one category over another? A daunting experience!

And, no, the merchandise didn't arrive all at once. In fact, some never came at all. I never knew for sure how the orders would come in. A shipping strike or the quota system for cotton imports could interfere. If there weren't enough orders for a specific garment, the manufacturer might decide not to cut it at all, but fail to notify those who had placed an order and were expecting it. The dye lots might not match or the ship date might be as much as two or three months off my plan. That would leave us with the sweater and shirts sold out by the time the planned skirts and pants arrived, for which we then had no tops available. The budget per category could thus be totally off by the end of the shipping season. The whole sweater shipment from one vendor might be delayed, due to off-shore cotton quota problems until well after the appropriate season, meaning that the store might be short sweaters during the whole buying season. I quickly learned to always have a back-up plan in reserve and to use off-price buying to supplement the stock for the store, as needed.

Confusing? Well, buying for a clothing store is kind of like being led in a dance when you don't know any of the steps and have no sense of rhythm and two left feet! And, yes, it is disconcerting – not for the faint of heart!

At the end of each season, however, manufacturers have to quickly unload any leftovers caused by credit problems, returns, and/or over-cutting. They are often eager to give a good markdown so that they can pay their factor, from whom they've borrowed for that season. A savvy retailer can often fill in their stock at great cut-rate prices, giving them additional profit if they are able to sell the merchandise at full retail.

Tricks of the trade, you might say.

I valued my newfound friendship with Mimi Lawrence, owner of Mimi's on Union in San Francisco, who I met through an off-price buying group. After that first meeting, we often met in San Francisco, shared cabs to and from the airports, and enjoyed sharing a room at the Figueroa Hotel during Market Week in Los Angeles. As struggling entrepreneurs, we benefitted not only each other's company, but also shared information about vendors and new lines, as well as expenses.

Uno Thomasson, the concierge at The Fig, always made us feel most welcome by giving us the same large room on the 2nd floor, when he learned about my fear of fire. We found it especially convenient because we never had to wait for the slow elevator, which was often belabored by busloads of Japanese guests of the hotel. Johnnie Circado, a waiter at the hotel knew me by name each time I came, and often supplied a little waiter magic for me with a cup of coffee and apple pie while I worked on my orders.

As it turned out, finding people to work in the clothing store was even easier than I would have imagined. Most were wives of University professors and doctors, valued and excellent salespeople, but also among my best customers and advertising, always using their 20% discount to good advantage – theirs and mine!

Pauline Worth, a color consultant, brought her expertise to the store several days a week. She analyzed colors and helped her clients find clothing to update their wardrobes in complementary colors and styles.

I became enthralled with the color analysis concept as I noticed how some styles of clothing seemed to sell more quickly in one color than another. What I was learning about the seasonal color harmony seemed relevant to both selling to the customer and buying at market. I began to write a training manual for my staff with input from Pauline and Irene Kennedy, who also worked part time in the store and who trained under Suzanne Caygill, the Grande dame of color analysis in San Francisco.

I had my colors analyzed by a total of eight people, including Caygill, over the next few months. I put into practice my newfound knowledge, as I bought for the store. I developed a color-style-harmony coding system for my purchase orders so that I would have clothing suitable for all of the 'seasonal types' each season. We organized the store in the same way. I was convinced that there was a definite color/style connection and that a savvy retailer could capitalize on what was seemingly innate.

Tarika became known for caftans, such as the one pictured below that features molas, the reverse appliqués from the San Blas Islands off the coast of Panama.

The Color Connection: From a Retailer's Perspective

I needed a training manual for my staff for this new system. The training manual evolved into somewhat more than an outline for what I eventually turned into a full-length book, The Color Connection: From a Retailer's Perspective. Not able to find adequate time to really immerse myself in writing, while working in Davis, I took my computer to our Ashland home for an extended "vacation" – a few weeks alone in January and February of 1985, after which I came back with an unedited draft. Jeanne Larsen painstakingly read and proofread the manuscript, as did Ed's mother, Florence, and his Aunt Harriet. All were most helpful in editing out most of those niggling errors.

Irene Kennedy pored over magazines, looking for samples of photos and illustrations, which we annotated and gave to JoAnn Stabb of the Design Department at University of California-Davis, who agreed to illustrate the book. She would deliver her sketches, and Irene and I would then critique them for hair styles, facial characteristics, and all of the things that go into making up the design of each of the seasonal types, so that the book would reflect the obvious differences that exist in the real world. Aware that some of the color books already seemed dated, we also tried to create a book with classic designs so that it would be as timeless as possible. As I look at it today, we achieved that goal. It is as fresh as it was when it was first published.

Tom Deininger, a local photographer who took photos for my advertising in the Sacramento Magazine since Tarika began, agreed to photograph models for the book. We carefully went through our customer list, searching for people who were typical of the various seasonal types. In the process, I discovered how difficult it really is to attribute categorically the types, which led me to better describe the 'connections' with a graphic chart. (The Color Connection: From a Retailer's Perspective, Winterspring Press. Pg. 34. http://webspace.cal.net/~callaway/tarika/Color.html)

."Just as the four seasons are on a continuum, I like to think of the seasonal harmony types on a continuum – from the late

autumn/early winter, when there are still a few autumn leaves around and the weather can't quite decide what it's going to do; mid-winter, alternating between persistent gray fog or rainy days to crisp snowy days that seem to encompass all the shades between white and black with very little color, perhaps a few red berries...." – The Color Connection: From a Retailer's Perspective

This graphic provided a way for me to legitimatize the variations found among the people labeled 'winter' by color analysts – people who had variations in their coloring and their visual design. I, for instance, was called a 'winter' by all but one of the color analysts, with Suzanne calling me an 'onyx winter,' which in my context would probably be a winter, but with autumn overtones.

This graphically explains my love for ethnic clothing and the texture of hand-woven fabrics, while retaining the personality characteristics and colors of the winter type.

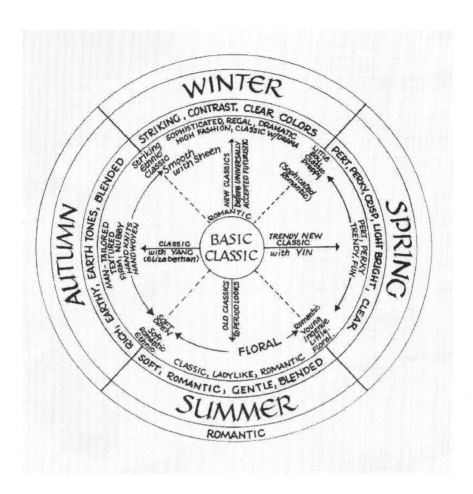

137

Pioneer Days: Spring, Summer, Autumn, and Winter types, stereotypically

Contemporary: Winter, Spring, Summer, Autumn styles

Typical hair style, accessory preferences

I self-published the book, hired a publicist, and began the promotion of the book through radio and TV interviews, but primarily through presentations and book signings at clothing markets in L. A. and San Francisco, as well as for clients of wardrobe and personal style consultants.

With a department store scheduled to open in the new 'Pig' Marketplace, so designated because of a ceramic and mosaic pig sculpture, and a Woodland Mall expansion just a few minutes away, I feared the worst. About this time a neighboring store, Jeff's Camera, closed their doors; Davisville Travel, our next-door neighbor, decided to move into their space and expand. That left an opening for an addition to my store if only we could cut through an existing wall. It turned out to be architecturally possible with only an arch and a step, or a ramp, to the somewhat higher elevation.

In anticipation of a downturn in business, unless I did something dramatic, I decided to double the space and focus on the theme of my book and the current color analysis fad. In fact, one of the chapters in the book is entitled: Fad, Fact, or Fiction? I actually believe it was a fad based on fact.

We decorated the new part of the store with pink, sage, and white floral, bouffant drapes at each dressing room door in contrast to the louvered ones on the autumn/winter side. White wicker furniture in the small waiting area at the front of the store provided a spring/summer-like look to coordinate with the type of clothing that would be found in that part of the store. Tarika, which had always been a somewhat unusual store, in that it had an interesting mix of ethnic, career, sportswear, and even jeans for the college crowd, now had a niche in the marketplace. Here was a place where those who had their colors analyzed could find clothes purchased especially for them - and where they could get professional help in interpreting their color cards.

Joanne Chiofolo had been my favorite hairdresser for several years. When she developed an allergic reaction to several of the products she used, I enticed her to come to work as my manager at the first Tarika. She had a natural style and ability to work with people. When Joanne left to be the Clinique representative at Macy's, I was fortunate to hire a series of talented and dependable managers, including Sue Cello, Susanna Waldrop and Kathie Klenzendorf. Carolyn Cole managed the finances and Betty Brown the "back-room" crew, checking in new merchandise, as well as tagging, and steaming. Without them I could never have considered opening another Tarika.

Beth Martinez, a rare and unexpected talent, did window displays, often using our gigantic stuffed toy bear as the focal point and inspiration. I purchased the bear at market, hoping to use it for a time as a prop in the window and then eventually to sell it. Little did I know what a fixture it would become! Beth turned that bear from a cheerleader to a coach, a laundress to a hairdresser - you name it, our talented bear could adapt!

One day though, a young man, who had watched the bear's changing persona with his girlfriend as they took nightly walks down Second Street during the past couple of years, asked to buy it. I was at a loss. We weren't sure we wanted to sell it by that time – and how to come up with a price. I explained. "This bear is invaluable – so experienced – it's priceless!" He agreed, but said it had such sentimental value for him and his fiancée that he wanted to give it to her as a surprise for graduation.

I finally cited an exorbitant price for the grizzled ol' bear that kids had been climbing over for the past three years. "Surely that will dissuade him." Saddened, the manager took his check for the outrageous price, rueful she would have to tell Beth and me that we no longer had a mascot.

The children were not the only ones saddened at this loss. The staff was bereft!

Sean and Lisa read to bear on one of its home visits

Not long after expanding the Davis store, I opened a second Tarika in a cottage on J Street in Sacramento. Marion Sulsona and Janie Mircetich, who had worked in the Davis store, now provided reliable stalwart support in the new store.

Marion reminded me the other day of the time a young man came in looking for clothes. We naturally assumed he was buying a gift. As it turned out, he confidentially told us they were for him. He was embarrassed to use the dressing rooms while we had other customers, so we stayed open in the evenings for him. Sacramento opened our eyes to many things. Ed and I both remember the many times I got a call in the middle of the night from the alarm company that we'd had a break-in at the Sacramento store. I'd get up, get dressed and rendezvous with the police, who would stay with me until the windows got boarded up. Eventually, a police car that just happened to be parked in the next block spotted and arrested a grab-and-run couple as they made another attempt.

The best way I found to market Tarika turned out to be the presentation of fashion shows and scarf demonstrations at restaurants in Davis and Sacramento, the Senior Center, and for various special events sponsored by organizations. The Scarf Wizard was a frequent presenter. Our models became, or already were, our best customers. My book, *The Color Connection*, presents a good catalog of our customers – in color photos taken by Tom Deininger. I used the photos of our customers along with their testimonials in my advertisements.

I published an almost monthly newsletter, partially because I like to write, but mostly because it was an excellent vehicle for telling my customers about new merchandise, as well as a way to keep our name in front of our customers. To this day, people remind me of recipes they got from the newsletter, which they still make and enjoy.

Crab Canapés

8oz. package of butterflake refrigerator rolls
8 oz. can water chestnuts, sliced
Combine the following ingredients:
7 ½ oz. can crabmeat
1 Tbsp. green onions, chopped
4 oz. shredded Swiss cheese
½ cup mayonnaise
¼ tsp. Curry powder
1 tsp. Lemon juice

Separate the butterflake rolls into three pieces, making 36 pieces in all. Place on greased baking sheet. Spoon on crabmeat mixture. Top with water chestnut slice. Bake at 400 degrees for 12 minutes. Serve hot. May be reheated. (Note: Make plenty because I've seen guests follow a tray of them around the living room like starving vultures!)

This continues to be one of our favorite hors d'ouevres, although I haven't seen butterflake rolls in a long time. We've learned to adapt! A flaky biscuit will do.

French Strawberry Pie (from Linda Troy, one of my employees)

1 pre-baked pie shell
1 large package of cream cheese
1 qt. Fresh strawberries
1 cup sugar
3T. cornstarch

Spread cream cheese that has been blended with a small amount of cream or milk into previously baked and cooled pie shell. Wash and stem berries. Arrange one half of berries with hulled side down. Mash remaining berries. Bring to boil. Slowly add sugar and cornstarch that have been mixed together. Simmer for about ten minutes, stirring as it thickens. Spread over uncooked berries in pie shell. Chill. Serve with whipped cream.

Changing Times

In the late 1980's my customer base began to change in subtle ways. My younger customers were buying homes for the first time, and seemed to be spending their surplus money on redecorating and landscaping. My older customers now had children entering college; tuition, board and room, and travel expenses appeared to be eating up money they used to spend on clothing. The economy was forcing the major department stores to bring in private label merchandise and advertise on-going sales. Everyone seemed to be looking for a bargain during this economic downturn.

In order to increase my customer base, I advertised in Sacramento Magazine and also increased Tarika's exposure through fashion shows at various restaurants, accessory demonstrations in-store and on local TV news shows, as well as giving Head-to-Toe Terrific classes on illusion dressing through the Learning Exchange.

Head-to-Toe Terrific Workshop

...designed to help you learn to accentuate the positive, while getting control of your closet and your budget. Profit by your mistakes in this "information gleaning from closet cleaning" session by bringing in one to three "closet mistakes" for evaluation, Sat. Aug 13, 9 - 11 a.m. Pre-registration fee of $5 includes continental breakfast and all materials. Optional figure analysis available for add'l fee of $15.

Joan Callaway
Author, *The Color Connection*

All Things Right & Relevant
Tues-Sat 10-6 • Sun 12-4
1640 E 8th St., Davis 759-9648

Nikos Mikalis, designer of Nikos Handwovens from Ashland, Oregon,, introduced me to the idea of trunk shows. He would arrive with samples of all of his designs in various colors and sizes. He provided personal help to our customers. We took orders and they were then later delivered to buyer's specifications. The handwoven coats, suits and vests seemed expensive at the time, but I'm still wearing several of his timeless vests some twenty-five years later. A real bargain when you think of it in terms of the number of times worn – cost per wearing.

"Head to Toe Terrific"…that's what we all want to be. Right? And head-to-toe terrific doesn't say anything about how old you are, how much you weigh or how tall you are. It's a given. We all want to look younger, taller and thinner. Like Kay Ballard used to say: "I don't want to talk about my weight, 'cause I weigh a bunch. My top weight is one hundred and fifteen pounds - and I won't discuss my lower half!" And about age, well, like they say, "There are three stages of age – youth, middle age…and my, you look good!"

I made an entrance to these illusion-dressing demonstrations with off-black sheer stockings and polka dot or red shoes and then changed into plain black pumps. That simple change increased my apparent height by two inches. Then I would put on a long scarf and appear taller yet. (Men with their ties have known this trick for ages!)Then I'd remind my audience to look at the height and weight chart next time they went to the doctor. "You know what? If you're two inches taller, you can weigh ten pounds more!" Illusion – that's what it's all about - a mild form of deception."

I was a fashion retailer for over twenty years before I finally retired. By that time, I'd done hundreds of figure analyses. No one is perfect! We all want to look perfect, but sometimes the body just won't cooperate – legs too short, neck too long. Even the most beautiful fashion models have some little imperfection they wish to camouflage or correct.

And, of course, fashions change. Our ideas of beauty change. The body terrific yesterday may be passé today. Remember the 1950's and the latex panty girdle, which made a woman look as though she had one rounded, firmly packed derrière. Remember when every teenager wanted to look like Twiggy? Today those same teenagers would be headed to the plastic surgeon for a breast enhancement to keep pace.

Keeping pace, that's what I've been doing – keeping pace with trends of the times. Remembering that quote I received from a friend not long after Glen and Keith died: "Our only real security in life is our ability to change." [Publicity photo by Tom Deininger – 1985]

Willis, The Scarf Wizard, made regular visits to add whimsy as well as wizardry to our fashion shows and scarf demonstrations. Head wraps were his specialty – to wear these successfully, you must have a certain *je ne sais quoi,* which I clearly lacked.

Employees Suzanna Waldrop and Laura Gilmore modeled Tarika fashions during photo shoots for advertising, as well as at the restaurant upstairs over the bank.

Partners in Crime

Although I'd become very engrossed in my business and in writing my book, I had never lost touch with Nancy Keltner. I had met Nancy at a cocktail party given to introduce her and her husband, Dr. John Keltner to the Medical School community. At a glance, I knew she was someone I wanted on the board of the Mental Health Association, so before she got ensnared in some other volunteer post, I called her the very next day, asking her if she'd be willing to be my publicity chairman. "Oh, Joan, she said, "I don't know anything about that."

Not to be dissuaded, I said, "No problem, Nancy. It's easy – the 5 W's - who, what, why, when and where." And the rest is history. Nancy not only did an outstanding job as publicity chair, it led her to write the FYI (For Your Information) teen column for the Davis Enterprise. As a result, based on the success of that column, she wrote her own book: *If You Print This, Please Don't Use My Name.* About the time Nancy retired from editing her column, coincidentally, I was recruiting board members for the floundering Yolo Community Care Continuum.

Never let a good person stay idle for long – they'll be snapped up by someone else. An old Chinese proverb, I think.

"Oh, Joan," said Nancy, "What could I do? What do I know about YCCC?"

I pleaded with her, "Just for a short time, Nancy, until we can get it back on its feet. You can help with publicity. It's easy – who, what, why, when and where." Nancy laughed and then agreed. She'd heard me say that before and look where that had led.

This time a crisis at YCCC brought me back onto their Board of Directors with the express purpose of building the board. I had almost immediate success as everyone I contacted agreed to help reorganize YCCC. Neighbors Norma and Larry Rappaport, a long time customer Lucia Becerra, and Chris Motley, as well as Nancy

Keltner rounded out the board, each adding a special badly needed expertise.

This time it was the beginning of one fundraising activity after another, including a "Be a Friend" bumper sticker campaign and a Celebrity Review for YCCC.

Fundraising had been a long-standing dilemma for YCCC, in fact for all non-profit agencies in our County, and the need for additional revenue seemed to be increasingly necessary as traditional funding sources dried up. California was coming into the deepest recession in recent memory. At a fundraising committee meeting of YCCC in the fall of 1991, I suggested we revisit the idea of a business, such as a consignment shop I'd suggested thirteen years earlier – a business that potentially would grow each year.

I presented a business plan for an upscale consignment shop, formally at a YCCC board retreat in January of 1992, with a start-up budget of $20,000. The board agreed it was a good idea and that plans should proceed. With her usual eagerness and optimism, Nancy enthusiastically proposed that the vision be expanded. "All of the mental health agencies are in constant competition for board members and for funds. What if the store earned money not just for one agency, but for ten? Imagine the community support that would generate?" While it was disappointing to think of giving up the projected revenue for YCCC, which was desperately needed at the time, the board could see the potential of Nancy's idea.

For the next few weeks, as Nancy traveled with her husband to medical meetings, she checked out consignment shops across the country, bringing home many fashionable "finds" to demonstrate further what an up-scale consignment shop could bring to Davis and Yolo County. .

Within days, Nancy and I met with the Executive Directors of the agencies we'd earmarked as potential recipients of the largesse we anticipated this venture might amass. After examining our business plan and projections, they had several comments:

"If it's such a good idea, Joan, why aren't you doing it as a profit-making business?"

"It's a generous offer, Joan, and we know it is something that you could organize and manage, but what if you die?" fittingly from the Executive Director of Hospice.

We answered the first question by saying, "One of the reasons it will be such a big success is because it is to be run by volunteers with the profits going to the agencies. As a for-profit business, it would probably still be a success, but not the win-win this is sure to be." And, of course, I blithely answered the second question with, "It's not IF I die, but when. If I do my job right, this new venture will take on a life of its own." Remembering what Glen always said about an administrator, "If he's doing his job the way he should, he is not indispensable."

The Executive Directors were enthusiastic, but didn't feel they could make any financial contribution since their agencies were already feeling the pinch of cutbacks from funding sources. Nancy and I, not to be deterred by a mere $20,000 scarcity, called some of the movers and shakers of Davis and together we organized, applied for non-profit status, and started the mother of all fund raising efforts, at least in our experience.

Bob Dunning, a columnist for the Davis Enterprise, for some time had, in jest, called Davis the City of All Things Right and Relevant. We asked if we could name the store after his quip, made in reference to the City Council calling Davis a Nuclear Free Zone. Davis has since gained a national reputation for other tomfoolery, as well, such as the time the police cited a woman for snoring when she disturbed her apartment's next-door neighbors; her snoring violated the town's Noise Ordinance. More than once, Jay Leno and David Letterman made fun of the town whose people didn't want the potholes in an alley filled, because it would ruin their character. Another time, the town spent a small fortune, building a tunnel for toads under a newly constructed overpass, lest they get run over crossing the new street. The City of All Things Right and Relevant, indeed!

With my business experience, I knew that the name All Things Right and Relevant, besides being consistent with promoting the idea of recycling and reusing, while helping non-profit agencies – all things right and relevant – it would give us top billing in the phone book under "Consignment Services" and "Clothes Used". A real benefit in advertising.

Some of our earliest volunteers and board members for several weeks tagged clothes and prepared for the new shop in my living room.

We opened for business six months later. I closed Tarika, brought its props, computers and other equipment, as well as its remaining inventory to the new location, and managed the new business for two years before it took on a life of its own and I was no longer needed. Today the business is hugely successful and has donated over $300,000 to the non-profits since it began.

In addition, the program that evolved over the years at All Things Right and Relevant and its eventual "child", R & R Thrift, now offers what I envisioned when we first conceived of the idea of a consignment shop many years ago. It offers part- and full-time employment to several mental health clients, as well as a place to belong. In addition, it enhances the lives of its community of volunteers.

♠

About the time I left as manager of the store in 1995, the Board of YCCC elected me President once again. When I discovered a fiscal crisis in the agency, I took on the job of Acting Director of YCCC as a volunteer. After several months of helping YCCC recover from its crisis in fiscal mismanagement, we hired a new Executive Director and I retired, that time for real – or so I thought.

About that time, Marci completed medical school in Michigan and was accepted for her residence at UC Davis Medical Center in Sacramento. I began to look for a place for them to live. I soon discovered there were few homes in Davis in the rental price range Marci and her husband, Peter, felt they could afford – one that would accommodate their family of four. I did, however, find a duplex that would be suitable for Ed and me for the period of the residency. We proposed that we move into the duplex, taking only part of our furniture and belongings. Marci and Peter would move into our house, but pay the rent on the duplex for us.

Peter took an interim job as Director of the Mental Health Association, which was ideal as he could be "Mister Mom" as the need arose for their two children. And arise it did – the demands on the family of a Resident Physician are not exaggerated. I enjoyed the days I got a call asking, "Is the Infirmary open?" because it meant I got to spend some one-on-one time with one of my grandchildren. Another win-win!

After we moved into the duplex, I stopped by the small struggling neighborhood market. I noticed that its big display window was dirty, unkempt and needed attention. They needed help. I approached the out-of-town owners with a marketing proposal, which they accepted. I was to help them with advertising and promotion.

One of the first things I did was to get those windows cleaned out. Coincidentally or maybe serendipitously, I ran into an old customer, Flo Grossenbacher, who was teaching fourth grade at the neighborhood school. "Flo, would your class like to do an art project – food related – to decorate Ray's Market windows?"

Eagerly, she accepted the challenge, "Sure, Joan. When do you want it done?" Within a couple of weeks, the students mounted their art and we planned a reception 'Open House' for family and friends to view the new window. Flo's class did a unit on nutrition. The students had an opportunity to display their art work. Ray's Market got the publicity, and we had a party. Another win-win! I do like those.

Halloween came and I invited the same group of students to participate in a window-painting contest in the complex where the market was located. Then I organized 'Jumpin' at the Jive', a fundraiser for Allied Services for Kids (ASK), which included a dunking booth, popcorn, a fiddling group, the Putah Creek Crawdads, face painting and fun for all. Flo's class helped again. Another win-win!

As the Christmas holiday approached, I took a big basket of cookies over to Flo's class, along with a note thanking them and her, and a note: "Flo, if you have a student who needs help with reading, I'd be happy to do a bit of tutoring. Let me know."

When school resumed after the holidays, Flo called me and said, "Joan, I don't know where to begin. I don't have just one student; I've got at least four who are seriously at risk."

"Well, I can't take on four, Flo, but I'll bet I can find some other people like me who would be willing to help out." About that time, I saw an article in the Sacramento Bee, announcing an eight-hour class for prospective tutors for Smart Kids, a non-profit in Sacramento, involved with tutoring elementary aged students. I signed up.

In the meantime, Flo arranged for me to meet with the principal of her school, who agreed they had real need for a tutoring program at their school – and probably other schools had the same challenges.

I attended the Smart Kids class and one of the trainers agreed to come to Davis to give a session if I recruited some volunteers. Our first training at Patwin School included sixteen tutors, after which they each tutored two students twice a week. We pre-tested the students; a post-testing at the end of the semester showed a 1.5 grade level improvement.

The Be Smart tutoring program expanded to other schools and by the second year, we had eighty volunteer tutors, some retired people like me, but also college students and several who worked full-time and still managed to find a few hours a week to work with young children.

I developed a website entitled Tarika that was referenced by the Veg Source Homeschooling site and that outlined the Be Smart Program, its curriculum, as well as some tips for reading/writing and math. [http://webspace.cal.net/~callaway/tarika/Welcome.html]

I received the J. C. Penney Golden Rule Award and $1000 for the use of the program. But awards are nothing compared to the satisfaction one gets from watching the eyes of a discouraged child change from quiet desperation to delight as he is able to read and experience success in school.

Tipper Gore Visits R & R and the Farmhouse

Tipper Gore, who has made mental health her No. 1 priority, visited Davis on November 1, 1994, to learn about Yolo County's unique continuum of care for the mentally ill. Gore's Davis visit was her only public appearance in California that day. The Vice-President's wife first made a stop at All Things Right and Relevant. Local officials, state mental health representatives, and a few local mental health volunteers were invited to tag along as she saw the continuum in action. As President of YCCC, I was one of the lucky ones!

According to the National Institute of Mental Health, thirty million Americans suffer from a mental disorder during any single month. "One in four families is dealing with a mental health problem," Gore told the audience at R & R that day. Gore, who advised President Clinton on mental health issues and twice testified before Congress in an effort to require insurance companies to cover treatment for mental illness, argued that coverage should be on par with that of physical ailments and not treated as a frill. [Photo: All Things Right and Relevant Manager Judy DeCesare, me, Tipper Gore, F.A.N. President Ruth Shumway, Congressman and Vic Fazio.]

Following her public appearance, Tipper was driven with an entourage of Secret Service vehicles to YCCC's The Farmhouse, a home-like outpatient mental health facility out on County Road 96 in rural Davis. Accompanied by Vic Fazio, Cap Thomson and me, Gore visited with mental health clients for an hour, sitting in their living room and strolling out to the barn. She went right out into the field and planted some onion starters, patted a donkey and thoroughly enjoyed her interaction with the clients, who followed along telling their stories. This was no photo op!

The Farmhouse is a working farm, and clients – most of whom come from locked facilities prior to their entrance – are each responsible for the care of an animal. Clients stay a maximum of eighteen months and hopefully move on to at least a semi-independent living situation when they leave. We were delighted to have the opportunity to explain that all of the services offered by YCCC are under one umbrella – residential treatment facilities, a vocational work program, socialization centers, as well as independent living. Because all of the services are related in this way, they operate under one philosophy, placing an emphasis on social rehabilitation rather than a medical model of care. Also, because of this network of services, any client problems are recognized early.

"I just want to tell you how much I respect and admire you for what you have done here. There are many states that dream of having a continuum of care and you've done it," Tipper said. We could only gaze at her in admiration as she chatted so easily with the mental health clients at the Farmhouse. Her interest in them was genuine – she was a joy to watch. [Photo #1: Me. Mrs. Gore and Dr. Cap Thomson; Photo #2 Mrs. Gore with staff of The Farmhouse.]

A Two Red Rose Day

January 27, 2001

Something must be up. Ed has taken the day off to celebrate my birthday with me.

My first clue was when he said, "I'll take you to lunch at Fusions at 1:30." A specific time? How strange. When at noon as we drove home from our grandson's basketball game, I said, "I'm hungry, Ed. Why don't we go eat now?" He put me off with, "I'll fix you an apple." As I rested with my feet up, he brought a plate full of cut-up apple, double cream blue cheese and crackers.

A nice treat, but that's rather strange for Ed. He's always ready to eat and we never decide the exact time we're going to lunch unless we are meeting someone. Besides 1:30's a little later than we might usually go to lunch anyway. Maybe he thinks we should have a late lunch, since we're not going to Marci and Peter's for bouillabaisse until seven tonight. No. I'll bet Jeanne and Michael, our friends from up in the foothills, will be waiting for us at Fusions. Well, that'll be fun. We haven't seen them for awhile. I won't spoil their surprise. I won't say a word.

I was ready at 1:30, but Ed continued to stall. Now since we were quite a bit later than the agreed upon time, I began to think that Jeanne and Michael weren't going to be waiting for us after all. Otherwise, Ed would have been more eager to arrive at the specified time.

At 2 p.m. Ed rolled my wheelchair down the long aisle of the restaurant. (I'd just a few weeks before had my second knee replacement, still wasn't walking long distances.) As we rounded the corner, I came face to face with a table full of "Surprise!" and a chorus of "Happy Birthday."

I must have looked stunned when I saw my son, Mark, big as life! He had called me not two hours before from his home in Corvallis, Oregon, (or so I had thought) to give me an update on Kristina, his oldest daughter. She had suffered what could have been a serious injury on a mountain trip the day before – one of her classmates had been fatally injured.

And there was Val, my oldest daughter, who also had called me just hours before from her home in Irvine, saying how sorry she was that she wasn't going to be able to make it up for bouillabaisse. She told me that my son-in-law Mike was driving up later from a meeting in the Bay Area, though. The whole family – Mark, Val, Marci, Peter, Chelsea and Max, Laurie, Jim and Connor – all seated around the table at Fusions!

As lunch was coming to a close, I asked Peter, "How was your meeting this morning, Peter?"

"Huh? Oh, just school," he said, looking a little bewildered. Later, he wondered why he had not just thought to say, "Oh, I wasn't at any Leadership Conference. I was picking these guys up at the airport." Instead, he acted a bit standoffish about the whole thing..."Just school stuff!" I thought he just wasn't very talkative. "Where can I get saffron?" Peter asked, trying to draw my attention away from his wife's excuse for why he hadn't been at Max's basketball game and diverting my attention to our planned bouillabaisse dinner.

Everyone laughed when I retorted, "From Mark," since I had given Mark a 'lifetime supply' of saffron from King Arthur's Flour for his birthday the previous May. We all agreed we'd meet back at Marci and Peter's for bouillabaisse at 7 p.m., and Ed rushed me out to the car so I wouldn't get chilled. The others stood gathered on the sidewalk in front of Fusions, chatting companionably, no doubt plotting the rest of the day and evening.

Later I suggested to Ed, as we were getting ready to go over to the Reilly's, "I think I'll make some garlic butter spread for the Italian bread I made yesterday. It would go great with the bouillabaisse, don't you think?" Ed replied, a bit impatiently, "Joan, it's your birthday. You don't have to take anything!"

"Okay! Okay!" I said.

There were a lot of cars on Elmwood when we arrived, but I didn't think much of it. Ed rolled my wheelchair up the driveway to the front door. When the door opened, my mouth flew open for the second time that day. What a crowd of people – Janis, who used to work for me and her husband, Steven – almost like family; Adela, who took care of me this past year when I had a foot tendon repair and then for my knee replacement recuperation.

So many people, many of whom I hadn't seen for years -- friends who used to come to our Christmas parties at this same house: the Quick's, The Walters, The Wisner's, my Centering and Tarika employees, and so many more. I was so surprised to see Joe and Mary McKenzie from El Cerrito, our Berkeley Rep buddies and long-time friends. Neighbors Merry and Vic Burns (Merry was my partner when we first opened Centering). My niece, Lisa and 2-year-old great-grandson Calvyn, who arrived from Eureka, too late for lunch, were also there. Ed's niece, Mariflo, and the other Hudson girls, Katie and Baby Anna, from the Bay Area were seated in the living room. Kit and Ken, a couple from Sacramento with whom we had just become friends greeted us. One surprise after another -- Ross Quick, Tim Magill; Ramona, Jim and their new twin babies, Hunter and Piper, cleverly named for planes since their parents are both airline pilots.

I moved from room to room the rest of the evening, talking with people, some of whom I hadn't seen for five and in some cases as many as ten years. They were people who spent many hours with me in that house, who enjoyed connecting with each other this night, too. I was suddenly very grateful Marci and Peter had decided to buy the Elmwood family home when Marci finished her residency. We designed the house and had it built in the early 70's – and as I looked at the various friends, it was like reminiscing when going through an old photo album. So many happy memories!

The invitation had specified no gifts, but a table full of flowers, wine, and cards from people who came and those who could not be there stood on a table along with a guest book. Among those who could not attend were Cap and Helen Thomson. Helen, a member of the California Assembly, sent a signed and sealed proclamation from the California Assembly, proclaiming January 27, 2001 to be Joan Callaway Day in the 8th Assembly District of the State of California, in honor of my 70th birthday!

California State Assembly

Certificate Of Recognition

PRESENTED TO:

Joan Callaway

Happy 70th Birthday
Wishing you
Good Health & Great Happiness

Proclaiming January 27, 2001
Joan Callaway Day
In the 8th Assembly District
State of California

MEMBER OF THE ASSEMBLY
CALIFORNIA STATE LEGISLATURE

The dining room table was laden with hearty hors d'oeuvres, catered by The Mustard Seed. No bouillabaisse! My wonderful friend and student, Adela, unable to observe the no-gifts edict, brought my favorite flan and pumpkin roll for the guests. My granddaughter Chelsea served beverages and cake from a bar in the kitchen area. Several people suggested, "Tell the kids -- this should be an annual tradition – just like the Christmas parties used to be, or at the very least again in ten years for your eightieth!"

As I sat in front of the fireplace, with friends, one after another, coming up to chat, someone appeared at the door. I gasped as I recognized the costume of a Madrigal singer – the finishing touch to what had already been a perfect birthday. An octet from the Davis

High School Madrigal Choir came through the door, singing "Happy Birthday"! When they had taken what was to be their final bow after a 20-minute concert, I told them why their appearance was so meaningful to me, and probably to many of the other guests.

"My son, Mark, sang with the 'Mads' for his whole high school career. Every year from 1971 – 1975, they performed at our Christmas parties. Under the direction of Dick Brunelle, they gathered at the Walters' house up the street, strolled caroling down Elmwood to our house, through the front door, and up the spiral staircase to sing on our balcony overlooking the living room. Dick and the choir afterward joined us for refreshments and carols, with Dick at the keyboard. I have such fond memories of those times…and that tradition."

The group, obviously moved by my story, asked if they could sing a couple of Christmas carols for us. It was January 27th, so the Christmas carols would be late or early, depending on your perspective. Dick Walters, whose daughter had been in the choir with Mark, asked if they would sing "Wassail, Wassail," one of our all-time favorites. After that and a rousing modernized version of "We Wish You a Merry Christmas," they asked if they could go up to the balcony to sing the "most beautiful song in the world, Ave Maria," which they were planning to sing before the Pope at the Vatican the following summer. They appreciated how much different the acoustics are for the singers and for the audience from that upstairs balcony. It was truly lovely.

As I came in the door earlier that evening, awed by the faces before me, Marci had placed some flowers in my arms as one person took my coat from me, another offered me a drink, and yet another advanced to give me a hug.

Lovely chaos in my mind, an abundance of riches – many friends and most of my loved ones here with me.

I barely noticed anything other than that I had been handed flowers -- not from whom they came nor what kind of flowers they were. It was only later, at home, when I removed the roses from the green paper wrapping to put them in a vase, that I realized that inside were 'two red roses with ferns and baby's breath.' I needed no card to tell me from whom they came. Two red roses are by far the sentimental favorite of Marci and are recognized symbolic by most of the Snodgrass clan. Valerie told me later that after everything else she'd done in preparation for this party, Marci had made one last stop

164

to add two red roses to the ice in the back of the van. She knew what they would mean to me.

Each time I receive these particular flowers, I'm reminded of a precious love, a priceless caring, and a time when we asked ten-year-old Keith, lying in his hospital bed after an appendectomy, "May we bring you something, Keith?" Keith answered in his very best Poor Pitiful Pearl voice, "Oh, maybe two red roses?" Two years later the family agreed to place just two red roses at the front of the church for his memorial service...and two nights later in the same church for the service of his father.

As I got ready for bed after the party, I looked at the two red roses on my dresser and had a little memorial service in my mind for Keith and for Glen. Glen would be so proud of his family as they've grown. We've all grown up well.

We are who we are because of him and the lessons we learned from that 'ill wind.' I'm pleased to be able to say, "He'd have been honored to have called the man our grandchildren call "Poppa," -- Ed, my husband of nearly twenty-five years (now nearly thirty five as I do the last editing) -- his friend."

Indeed, it was a "two red roses" day! A day to remember and to cherish!

The Madrigal Choir octet sang from the balcony at my 70th birthday party.

The family gathered the next morning for brunch at our Villanova house:
Standing are Peter Reilly, Granddaughter Lisa Henry, Katie Hudson with Baby
Anna, Mark, Mike Henry Ed, Laurie & Jim Wheeler; Seated: Val with Connor
Snodgrass and Calvyn Henry, me with Chelsea Reilly, Marci with Max Reilly

No Way to Make Sense of the Senseless

From my journal entries – September 11-13, 2001

I was checking my e-mail when our nephew, Ryan, who had been scheduled with Ed for a flying lesson on the morning of September 11, 2001, called to ask if we had heard that terrorists had struck the World Trade Center. Ed said he had just heard it on the radio. I immediately switched on Channel 10 to a surreal scene as they replayed the tower mushrooming to the ground followed by a devastating fire in the financial district of New York City – a scene that looked more unreal than the special effects of a movie.

It fascinates me, in this age of television shows and movies, how we have come to depend upon dramatic clues to interpret events - how the narrative line slowly builds, how the background music is ominous, hinting toward danger, and then climaxes in some powerful event. That Tuesday morning, no screenwriter had done his homework, no composer had thought to point toward anything significant. There was no narrator or pundits to make sense of the senseless.

Silently, and as if in slow motion, a plane flies into a 110-story tower; flames leap and smoke billows; debris scatters; different free lance photographers deliver yet another camera angle. It becomes even more surrealistic as the screen is divided and the right half shows a smoking Pentagon; Peter Jennings announces a fourth plane has crashed in a Pennsylvania field, their efforts to attack the White House or Camp David apparently thwarted by rebellious heroic passengers. Our President, wisely, by this time is sequestered in an underground bunker in the heartland of our country.

This movie doesn't make sense. I sat for hours motionless, transfixed before that large screen as it began to sink in fully – this is not a War of the Worlds movie, not a game, but a real life attack. And it was happening now, and I was numb, unbelieving. When the towers fell again and again, hour after hour, rerun after rerun –an agonized voice rose from within me, "Can this really be happening?"

Now, two days later, like the debris from those scenes of horror, my thoughts also are still flying, falling, settling, like a pile of rubble that still must be sifted for meaning. Like the rescue workers searching for survivors and the FBI searching for clues, my search for meaning will take a long time.

Now, only two things I know for sure. One is the profound grief I feel for those who died, those who were injured, all of those families who did not see their loved ones walk through the doors of their homes that night. A few hours passed and the reality hit that this terror was designed to strike at me, at the heart of every American.

I left a message on the cell phone of my son, Mark, who often travels across the country on business. "I hope you are at your desk, Mark...Please call." Later that day, it was comforting to hear his voice, as well as that of each of the other children, who soon called to ask how I was doing. I could only report, "I am filled with grief for the victims of this horrific attack.

For the past several days the middle school student I am helping to homeschool has been studying the Middle East and the U. S. /Israeli refusal to participate in the Conference on Racism. We had been reading the news and discussing the Middle East conflict. We suddenly have a new appreciation of what life must be like for those around the world who live daily with terrorism and constant unrest in their communities.

How can we ever hope to repair the world when issues that face us are so far reaching and complex? How can we ever hope to heal when we already hear talk of war – of acts of revenge and retaliation that may threaten the lives of other innocent people.

As many people from countries far and near sent messages of sympathy and disbelief that something like this could happen in the U. S., the TV coverage showed Arabs cheering, perhaps speaking for many with, "Do you get it now?"

Do you get now what it is like to live with constant threats of imminent violence, the ever-present anxiety and danger and fear that many people live with daily, not only in Israel, but also in Bosnia, Northern Ireland, Afghanistan, all over the Middle East? How we in America have taken our freedom and peace for granted! Yes, now I am beginning to get it.

The second thing I know for sure is I have a sudden overwhelming admiration and appreciation for the firefighters, police officers, rescue workers, and countless others who have lent a hand, offered help, comforting the victims, donating blood, putting their

168

dedication to service to others before their own welfare. Each and every one is a hero today.

I'm reminded of a story I received some time ago about a man and his daughter saying goodbye at the airport with the phrase, "I wish you enough..." When asked what that meant, the man said it was a wish that had been handed down in his family for generations. I share the sentiment:

I wish you enough sun to keep your attitude bright.

I wish you enough rain to appreciate the sun more,

I wish you enough happiness to keep your spirits alive.

I wish you enough pain so that the smallest joys in life appear bigger.

I wish you enough gain to satisfy your wanting.

I wish you enough loss to appreciate all that you possess.

I wish you enough hellos to get you through the final goodbye."

Sorting through this series of surreal events, through layers of rage, grief and blame, I realize that to gain further meaning and to fully appreciate the joys in life again will take time. And like the disaster workers sifting through the wreckage, in the end I don't yet know what else I will find in my search.

When you've lost a loved one tragically and abruptly, seeing a new tragedy like this unfold before your eyes sends you reeling. It isn't that I'm suffering flashbacks, although that acrid sick metallic taste of smoke seems to linger in my mouth when I see the flames light up the sky. It's the flash-forwards that are causing me to lie awake at night – flash-forwards to what the victims, the injured and uninjured survivors, families, friends, and colleagues of those who are missing are experiencing now and will have to endure in the near future. It is the concern that the saber rattling I hear will lead to random acts of retaliation, as well as all-out World War III.

My God. The horror. The heartache. Pain beyond all imagining.

Even my physical body remembers how it is to suffer this kind of emotional trauma. I walk around distractedly trying to keep busy and then I stop suddenly to weep. I watch television for a moment and turn it off. On and off. On and off. I can't bear to watch; I can't bear not to watch. I get the chills, followed by a feverish flush, followed by acute nausea. Much like when the numbness began to wear off and the horror and reality of Glen and Keith's last few hours really began to sink in after our fire. I wake at 3, 4, and 5 a.m., Glen and Keith's hospital rooms a vivid memory – flashbacks of the fire and its aftermath.

I seek to understand how these terrorists -- people who might have been our neighbors -- could have come to the point of abandoning their families, risking their lives for what must be solemn beliefs. What must their pain and suffering have been to get to this place? Is it like a cult who will follow their leader anywhere and in anyway?

As the media pundits call out for retaliation, few try to shed some light on what might motivate anti-U. S. sentiment in the Middle East. One exception was ABC's Jim Wooten, who reported that "Arabs see the U. S. as an accomplice of Israel, a partner in what they believe is the ruthless repression of Palestinian aspirations for land and independence." He continued, "The most provocative issues: Israel's control over Islamic holy sites in Jerusalem; the stationing of U.S. troops in Saudi Arabia near some of Islam's holiest sites; and economic sanctions against Iraq, which have been seen to deprive children there of medicine and food."

I believe it is so important to examine the highly contentious role of the United States in the Middle East in order to illuminate some of the forces that have given rise to this violent extremism. That, I think, would contribute far more to public security than do pundits calling endlessly for indiscriminate revenge. Violence is sure to beget more violence.

Posse justice resembling the "Wanted, Dead or Alive" posters of yesteryear as advocated today by our President will not resolve the situation – in the short or long term. It is my prayer that our leaders and the people across the country who are devastated by this attack will act like adults, not like children in a sand pile.

Although I am deeply saddened by what has happened, I plead with those responsible to deal with the perpetrators in a rational way that does not create more and long-lasting ill will and future retaliations. Arrest, trial, dialogue, negotiation, a degree of compromise over the issues that plague us – whatever it takes to be responsible in our efforts to seek those guilty and not threaten the lives of more innocent people for the sake of proving our might.

Two wrongs never make a right. Like the children in the sand pile, I think we need a lot of adult supervision right now. Are there enough adults?

I wish you enough adults…

I wish you enough…

Poppa

Time and time again, Ed has proven that I'm a discriminating "picker" of husbands. For better or worse? The betters far outweigh the "worse." He's a keeper! He rises to whatever challenges we encounter with grace and generosity. He's always there for everyone, from "Pop, can you come get me? Could you drive me to my game?" to "Ed, my computer's not working. Could you take a look at it?" He always rises to attend to events of more consequence, such as when Lisa, away at college, had a strangely disconcerting seizure. Ed flew over to Eureka in one of his planes and brought her back to Davis for a bit of R & R before flying home commercially to her parents in Irvine, California.

This week as we leave for a week in Ashland, four hours and forty –five minute drive from our house, he said, "You know, there's no reason we couldn't see your sister on our way…drive to Eureka, stay overnight with Sean and then drive on the next day to Gold Beach. Would you like to do that?" That's about nine hours out of our way, so, like I said…he's a keeper!

With a memory like a steel-trap, at the drop of a hat, he can and does come up with a pertinent quip, pun, or funny story he's reminded of. Our second-generation grandchild now asks him to repeat once again a story Ed told to his mother, Lisa, as well as to each of the other grandchildren at the appropriate age: the traditional Wide Mouthed Frog story. At each of the capitalized parts of the story, Ed's mouth gets wider than one would believe it could.

Once upon a time a WIDE MOUTHED FROG lived in a pond. One day, while swimming around the pond he met a stork. "HI, MISTER STORK, WHAT DO YOU EAT?" said the WIDE MOUTHED FROG. "I eat the little fishes that live in the pond", said the stork. The WIDE MOUTHED FROG said, "THAT'S VERY INTERESTING". After swimming on a little more the WIDE MOUTHED FROG met a hippopotamus. "HELLO, MR. HIPPOPOTAMUS, WHAT DO YOU EAT?" said the WIDE MOUTHED FROG. "I eat the vegetation that grows on the bottom of the pond", said the hippopotamus. The WIDE MOUTHED FROG said, "THAT'S VERY INTERESTING". Swimming along a little more, the WIDE MOUTHED FROG met an alligator. "HELLO, MR. ALLIGATOR, WHAT DO YOU EAT?" said the WIDE

MOUTHED FROG. "I eat wide mouthed frogs!" said the alligator. The WIDE MOUTHED FROG said, "That's very interesting."

And, of course, Ed's mouth gets smaller than you would believe it could get when he says the last line.

Nearly every birthday or Christmas, one of the grandchildren gives Ed some rendition of the wide mouthed frog, such as a framed mirror in the shape of a frog, a soft velvety stuffed frog with crown and scepter, or a cast iron pencil holder. As his collection of frogs grows, typically Ed, he says, "Too bad I didn't tell them the story of King Midas!"

Granddaughter Kristina telling the wide mouthed frog story to a cast iron wide mouthed frog Ed had just received as a Christmas gift.

Paul Newman & Robert Redford, Watch Out!

An old man, dressed in a clapping-hands BRT tee shirt under a blazer, limped onto the Berkeley Repertory Theatre on a Sunday afternoon with assistance from one of the ushers. He allayed our fears, "I'm not here to tell you to turn off your cell phones and open your cellophane-wrapped candies now." And about that time, a cell phone tune began to chime. Of course, it was his. This was Geoff Hoyle at his best. He commended the sponsors of the play and then chatted on for several minutes, winking at the audience now and then, as he explained how valuable the BRT membership is. He then told us that everything on the stage would be auctioned off after the performance, even the gargantuan replica of the Eiffel Tower. All by way of introducing his translation and adaptation of Georges Feydeau's farce, *For Better or Worse*, directed by David Ira Goldstein, which would continue playing through April 24th on the Thrust Stage.

Moments later, of course, by donning a smoking jacket Geoff transformed the "old man" into the young husband of a most pregnant wife, in labor a month early with their first child. The play has all the components of the classic farce: the unhinged husband, his wife, a constipated brat, a military contract for unbreakable chamber pots, the potential contractee, his wife, and her lover, as well as a pert, but not too bright, maid.

But wait! That's not even the best part. After the first act, Geoff again in his old man outfit gives a mini-lecture about "door slammers", as this type of farce is known to professionals. A young man, ostensibly only recently arrived from Paris (remember the replica of the Eiffel Tower that towers over the stage), brings out a door and holds it. Geoff explains that we are not to notice him – he is an invisible "hinge."

Then he asks those in the audience who are members to raise their hands. A fair number appeared to be subscribers. Geoff then says, "On rare occasions, subscribers have the opportunity to stand on the stage of BRT. Today is one of those days." He is clearly acting as though he is an old codger subscriber who is having one of those rare opportunities. He points down into the second row center at a young woman in a black and white striped sweater and invites her to use the step to climb up on the stage.

We assume that she is a plant.

But then he turns to our row and points directly at Ed, comments on his nice smile, and invites him to join them on the stage. Ed climbed over the two ladies at the end of our row and walked toward the stage. "If you're feeling athletic, you can just leap up or you can go down there to the step," Geoff quipped. Ed did the leaping up bit to applause from the audience.

It's a pretty gray-haired audience on Sunday afternoons, so his having the ability to "leap up" seemed commendable.

Now the purpose of this exercise became quite clear. "Since this door with the invisible 'hinge' can't possibly slam, we have a smaller version," he said. At which point an usher brought forth a small replica of a door, which COULD slam, and Geoff invited an elderly gentleman from the first row to come forward to be the door slammer.

Geoff hands Ed and the woman their scripts – very small cards, which they could palm in their hands. He then hands out the costumes – a translucent pink negligee, which the woman holds up in front of her and the ugliest black and green plaid trousers, which Ed holds up in front of his own black ones. "Now, let's have a little rehearsal," Geoff says, again winking and mugging toward the audience with a bit of a typical Geoff Hoyle bow. "Now, you're just to imagine these two are nude beneath their costumes."

They go behind the door in the middle of the stage, which is being held by the Frenchman, whom "we can't see." Geoff makes some comment to him and he says, "OUI" that sounded more like "WE!" The two 'actors' are guided behind the door for a rehearsal. The woman is first – she walks through the open space BY the door, as opposed to THROUGH the door. Geoff ad libs for five minutes about her error. She must go THROUGH the door and slam it behind her, at which time the gentleman at the small replica door is to SLAM the door, creating the noise for the scene. Then ED is to follow her through the door, "slamming" it behind him, and the gentleman door slammer will slam the replica, simultaneously - well, you get the picture.

So they try it again...this time the woman "opens" the door and goes "through", slamming it behind her and the gentleman creates the noise of the slam. When Ed gets on stage, Geoff instructs him to look out at the audience, not at the woman. The woman, holding the negligee in front of her is now instructed to be shocked at seeing Ed, say her one line, and drop her negligee. He reminds the audience that she is now nude, and that she should cover herself in embarrassment. She says her one line – "Victor," but is then reminded this is a French farce, so she says, "Victoire," to hoots from the audience.

So, now, "You must cover yourself," Geoff instructs. So, of course, she does…both arms, covering her breasts. Geoff is quick to point out that she is fully unclothed, so she now moves one arm to her right shoulder and the other to her left thigh. Never missing a beat, Geoff says, "Now she's covered all the important parts – her shoulder and her thigh." The audience is in an uproar at this point. This is a lot funnier than the play!

Geoff instructs Ed to now look over at the woman, say his line - "Yvette," but, of course, he's to get so excited that he drops his pants. Geoff reminds him that he is now nude. So he covers himself. Well, Ed had no trouble figuring out where to put his hands, but Geoff prodded him to acknowledge that his hands probably wouldn't be quite so close, aroused as he must be at seeing Yvette. So Ed put his crossed hands out a bit further...and then when Geoff looked askance, a bit further out, at which point Geoff said, "If it lasts longer than four hours…!" (By now, I'm hysterical. Tears run down my cheeks.) "…call 911."

At intermission, our friend Linda Brandenburger from Sacramento came over from across the theatre to ask Ed to sign her program, which he did – "Victoire!" She said, "I almost didn't come today. Glad I did, though. I wouldn't have missed this. But I couldn't decide which was more fun to watch – the stage or Joan, who was laughing so hard."

People kept asking if the participants had been planted in the audience. Others suggested that Ed would be up for a Tony. I just say "Watch out Paul Newman and Robert Redford – here comes Ed! I'm still laughing. Where was my camera anyway? You're not laughing? Well, maybe you had to be there.

Serendipity

"There was an old woman who swallowed a fly..."
Lyrics by Rose Bonne and made famous by Burl Ives.

"Your cholesterol is pretty high, Ed. I think we should start you on Lipitor and see if we can get it down," the doctor said to what appeared to be a perfectly healthy, then fifty-five year old white male. Ed swallowed the new medication faithfully.

Some time later, he said, "Doc, I've got these pins and needles in my feet – sometimes it's really painful. Anything we can do for it?"

"We should do some neurological tests; see if it is back related. But if it isn't, I could prescribe some Neurontin." The X-rays and neurological tests came back negative. Ed swallowed the Neurontin and Lipitor faithfully.

One day a few years later, Ed visited a new doctor, Paul Riggle at U.C. Medical Group in Davis, whom our daughter Marci had highly recommended. In the course of an evaluation, Dr. Riggle said, "You know I've read that Lipitor can sometimes cause this kind of peripheral neuropathy. Why don't you discontinue the Lipitor and try eating salmon twice a week and oatmeal every day for breakfast. See if we can keep the cholesterol down with diet – and, of course, exercise."

Well, as it turns out, the peripheral neuropathy presumably caused by the Lipitor is irreversible, but my husband Ed and I both got much healthier with all that salmon, oatmeal, and exercise. Or so we thought.

One day a couple of years later, Ed had a single episode of atrial fibrillation where the heart beat races out of control, the rhythm disorganized, rapid and irregular. He spent a few hours in the emergency room at Sutter Davis Hospital, where they prescribed Digoxin. He later saw a cardiologist, had stress tests and a complete cardio workup; no other heart problem was found. Even so, he was advised to continue the Digoxin.

Unfortunately, he mentioned the atrial fibrillation to his FAA approved doctor and his medical for flying was suspended. This meant he could no longer fly as Pilot in Command, drastically curtailing his teaching and examining of beginning and/or instrument pilots at Executive Flyers, the flight school he owns and operates in Sacramento. However, his primary care physician and his cardiologist both concurred that he was perfectly fit to fly even while taking the Digoxin, as it should have no impact on his ability. HOWEVER, in the process of the evaluation, the FAA discovered he was taking Neurontin, which, unbeknownst to him and his doctor, all along had been an FAA forbidden substance. His medical was again denied, this time because of the Neurontin. And are you ready for this? The FAA proclaimed that Neurontin is suspected of causing atrial fibrillation!

In the meantime, Ed developed a recurring nausea – one might well suspect because of stress of his imperiled career, but Dr. Riggle, his primary care physician said, "It could be one of several things, Ed. Most probably it is the Digoxin that is causing the nausea, but we should run some tests to be sure." In order to have his medical reinstated, Ed discontinued the Neurontin. In an attempt to get rid of the nausea - just in case - he stopped taking the Digoxin, but it would take several days before the medication was completely out of his system. The nausea continued. Blood work ruled out pancreatitis, which is often suspected with this kind of nausea. A CT scan was eventually scheduled.

Are you seeing why I thought of the old lady who swallowed the fly, the children's song Burl Ives made famous? High cholesterol indicates use of Lipitor. It is believed that Lipitor causes peripheral neuropathy. Neurontin is prescribed for peripheral neuropathy; Neurontin is believed to cause atrial fibrillation. Digoxin for atrial fibrillation caused nausea. Prolonged nausea was indication for doctor to order a CT scan.

Dr. Riggle told Ed, "The CT scan may well have been a life-saving procedure as they found a mass on your left kidney and ureter. You have an appointment to see an oncologist Monday morning."

Dr. Ralph Devere White, the oncologist, reassured Ed, saying that the tumor was probably benign because of the placement and size. However, it would have to be biopsied to be sure. Cystoscopy would be performed at the Surgery Center at the University of California Davis Medical Center (UCDMC), within a couple of weeks. The biopsy would then take five or six days.

Dr. Low performed the cystoscopy, took a biopsy sample, and implanted a stent. Fearing that I might be phoned by the surgeon's office regarding an appointment, Ed phoned me after the biopsy. He said that based on what Dr. Low had seen he believed the tumor malignant; the biopsy results five days later confirmed this visual diagnosis. Based on his findings, he scheduled Ed to meet with Dr. Ellison the following Monday to make plans for removal of the left ureter and kidney. "It looks as though it is an early stage carcinoma; our hope is that chemotherapy will not be necessary."

Serendipity, happy chance, or Lady Luck that it was found early. Serendipitous that he took that Lipitor all those years ago - and that he had a thorough doctor and an HMO that approved a CT scan for nausea!

The Long Wait

The day of the surgery was a day and a half! Well, it seemed like it. At 10 a.m., we arrived as requested at Tower One, Surgery Admission at UCDMC, where our daughter, Marci, did her residency and still practices. With his typical sense of humor, Ed had days before resurrected from the recesses of his memory an almost appropriate – apropos, I mean - limerick for the occasion, and typed it up. He's got one for EVERY occasion.

He packed a bag at Marci's urging – "your own toothbrush, slippers and a robe...you'll be glad you have them." And at the last minute before leaving home, he asked me to help him find a safety pin.

Finally, at 10:30 the nurse escorted Ed back to a room to get him ready to be taken up to surgery – two hours later. I waited in the lobby while he changed into his surgical gown, basically a length of print fabric with some inefficient and insufficient snaps and a couple of ties. Lounging leisurely and rather nonchalantly, I thought, Ed proudly pointed to the typed limerick he had pinned to the front of the skimpy green gown:

> There once was a man with a hernia,
> Who said to his doctor,
> "Gol' dern ya,
> When you work on my middle,
> Be sure you don't fiddle
> With things that do not concern ya!"

Marci ran errands, answered pages, and made phone calls, doing her best to distract us. And best of all, she borrowed a key to the OB call-room, where after a sustenance salad lunch in the hospital cafeteria, I was to rest comfortably while Ed was in surgery.

I entered the 'suite' where the 'attendings' – chief residents – spend any hours they can off the floor, catching a few winks or catching up on charts. The TV that barely worked if you unplugged the electric alarm clock didn't look particularly well used. There was a computer that apparently runs 24 hours a day and a bookcase with a two-year-old Better Homes and Gardens, several large OB tomes, and a medical compendium, offering proof that this room offers more than a quiet, private respite for the over-worked and often over-wrought house staff.

The suite had its own private bathroom – more than a restroom, as it was strangely larger than the bedroom – a huge walk-in shower, stacks of towels and wash cloths, toothpaste, special hand lotion for hands too often scrubbed, and even a lonely Tampax. Sterile and hospital-like, not a personal touch in sight, the room was just white tile and chrome.

I'm going on and on describing things just so you'll have to wait and wait as I did to hear the verdict, to hear how the surgery went. I actually slept for a couple of hours. Who'd have thought I'd be able to do that?

The anesthesiologist resident paged Marci as she had promised about 5 p.m. (about three hours into the surgery) – "The kidney's released. He's doing fine. It'll probably be about another hour and a half or so."

That time passed every so S-L-O-W-L-Y. Marci went out to run another errand, brought back some coffee, a couple of not-very-good eggrolls and a piece of truly decadent chocolate pecan pie from the cafeteria. While Marci was gone, I checked my yahoo.com e-mail, but couldn't remember the name and password we use at cal.net. I read a few of the N.Y. Times news articles and just dinked on the Internet to pass the time. After we'd eaten, Marci answered some of her pending e-mails from patients. I watched Jim Lehrer's News Hour – all the equivalent of pacing. Marci made several calls to see if Ed had arrived in the Recovery Room. Alas! No!

7 p.m.: At last, Marci's pager went off with a pager number to call. More waiting. Finally, Dr. Lars Ellison, the surgeon, called back. "The surgery went well. I didn't see anything I hadn't expected to see. I didn't see anything in the bladder or nodes. No great loss of blood. He tolerated the anesthesia well and looks like all he needs now is recuperation from surgery." He promised to look in on him Friday afternoon.

Marci predicted it would be another hour and a half or two before they sent him to his room. Well, first they didn't have a room ready for him...and then they were monitoring a low heart rate. No unauthorized personnel (read family!) are allowed in the Recovery Room at this hospital, but Marci had her Dr. Marci tag on, so they let her in. She found him to be very groggy as they'd given him morphine for pain. Back she came to report to me. I really didn't want to go home until I'd seen him myself, so even though the Recovery Room is restricted to staff in scrubs, Marci escorted me in. Not that I could do a thing! His mouth was dry, he was all wired up to a monitor, and it was not all that reassuring to hear the monitor beep every once-in-awhile when the heart rate dropped too low. But the RR staff assured us that this was not all that abnormal; they weren't very concerned and when we left at about 11 p.m., they were readying him for a transfer to his own room. Friday will be a better day – hopefully!

September 2004: Hooray! Three month visit to Dr. Ellison and the cystoscopic examination proved that the cancer has not returned. We're elated.

December 21, 2004: Unfortunately, cystoscopic examination today showed a tumor on wall of bladder. We decided not to tell the family until after Christmas by which time appointment with Dr. Devire White, bladder oncologist, will have been confirmed. We'll know more then.

January 24, 2004: Dr. Devire White performed resection of the bladder tumor. He suggested chemotherapy sessions as a preventive measure, one a week for six weeks.

March 11, 2005: Last of six chemotherapy treatments today. No nausea or any other systemic effects. Ed's optimistic good humor prevails, as he remembers the story about the man falling from the 12th floor of a building, now at the 6th floor, saying, "I'm O.K. so faaaer..."

June 21, 2011: I'm pleased to report that many subsequent cystoscopies, including one today, have been negative.

Ed Callaway
Designated Pilot Examiner
May 21, 2003
Sacramento Executive
Airport, CA

Glories, Gifts, and Graces

As I write this, all of my children have families of their own, bringing us the ultimate gift - grandchildren and even our first great-grandchild. Despite all the changes and growth, the memories of that fateful day still crop up from time to time, such as the two red roses – trigger points, little memorial services in my mind that probably will never cease to occur.

I still wear the teardrop necklace I had made up from the engagement and wedding rings of my first marriage. This small token reminds me of my twenty year marriage to Glen, which for some reason seems to have been a longer period than that of my second marriage to Ed – probably because it was during this time that all of our children were born. We experienced many moves and much growing during the nearly twenty years we were married. As we grow older, the time passes much more quickly – or so it seems.

Every once in awhile, a grown man, sometimes with a child in tow, will say something like, "Mrs. Callaway, I'm Todd. Remember me? Keith and I were buddies."

Oh, my! I do a brief double take as I think – he's a grown man! Time has passed so quickly. He must be fifty years old! I realize that I still see Keith in my mind's eye as a 12-year old. What a shock! I wonder what Keith would be like now at age fifty-two ...probably with a family? Does it hurt? Yes, a bit...but I quickly turn my thoughts to how nice to have been remembered by Todd, who felt confident enough to stop and talk with me; how well he seems to have grown up.

I'm in control of how I think about things now. At some point in my recovery, I realized I had a choice about how I reacted to those trigger points...to how I thought about things. For instance, I could think about some crazy, funny little thing Keith had done, perhaps riding madly down the street toward baseball practice wearing his striped T-shirt with his favorite baseball cap, mitt hanging from the handlebars. Or I could think of the thousand times I hadn't been a perfect mother, or I could dwell on the last time I saw him lying there unconscious in the hospital, never to speak to me again. That's still my choice!

Even today, though, I have not a good answer for that dreaded question: "How many children do you have?" How do I answer? Do I deny Keith? Do I say that I have four living children? It's a conundrum I've yet to solve satisfactorily.

Although without a doubt this was the most tragic, the most traumatic and significant turning point in my life, like everyone I've had others. I've experienced the sense of loss, as our parents grew older, suffering from illnesses, and then again at the permanent loss at their death. I've struggled with the adjustments that I've had to make, as I've grown older; although the mind still thinks of itself as thirty, the body is no longer willing. I've experienced the joys and the trials of childbirth and rearing, and ultimately the separation and giving up of parenting in favor of deep friendships as the lives of my children evolved into adulthood. I've enjoyed the joys and trials of owning my own businesses – first an art gallery, then gift/jewelry store, and eventually two women's clothing stores. I've written and published a book – another labor not unlike childbirth. And then retirement!

Everyone knew I wouldn't be able to just sit around and eat bon-bons and watch soap operas. I've always volunteered for something during all of the time I had the stores – Bereavement Outreach, Yolo Community Care Continuum, the Mental Health Association, and before retirement I helped to establish and run the upscale consignment shop to benefit 12 mental health agencies in our county. Retired! My husband scoffs, "You change directions every five years – a new store, a new career. I'm just glad it's not me!"

Believing that education is a lifelong pursuit, I'm always reading, always trying to find new and better ways to teach my students. This is not an interim period in my life. It's a significant stage in life. There are at least twenty books on my bedside stand, waiting to be read; there are twenty places I'd like to visit; twenty people I'd like to meet and get to know better, perhaps even twenty great-grandchildren.

It was almost forty years ago, I took a good look at my life. I pondered who I was - and more importantly, who I wanted to be and what I wanted to do with the rest of my life. It was sixty years ago that our country had a rude awakening about our role in world events that united us in a new found solidarity after the attack on Pearl Harbor – helped us to discover who we were and wanted to be as a country. It likewise took a major terrorist attack on the World Trade Center and the Pentagon on September 11, 2001 to arouse our consciousness to what much of the rest of the world has been experiencing for years. It took this crisis close to home to enflame our passions, to unite our country in purpose.

It is ironic that when all is going smoothly and our love, families, and/or land are secure, we tend to focus on insignificant problems that divide us; when we are threatened, we come together to look at the bigger picture - the promise, the possibilities, our true purpose in life. It is at this time of crisis that we have an opportunity to renew passions that have been kept slumbering as if in suspended animation. It is at these critical times we are able to risk, to go forward in the face of overwhelming odds, to search out the possibilities and the promise. It is out of crisis that we get the chance to be reborn, to choose the kind of change that will help us grow, to enable us to fulfill ourselves more completely – as individuals – or as a country.

It is the unending paradox that we learn best from crisis – from loss, pain, and suffering. It is through our grief that we are able to disengage ourselves from the day-to-day status quo and bring ourselves to fully examine our purpose – what is really important in life.

Perhaps crises can be seen as our homework, given not to oppress us, to beat us down, but to help us grow – to help us move on to the next stage of our life. It was important for me to find a new definition for who I was - something besides a survivor, a bereaved widow and mother. I feel lucky to have been able to turn tragedy into triumph – to feel worthy again - through helping others.

I have been rewarded in many ways:

California Mental Health Association - for Bereavement Outreach,
Two Bell Awards from the Mental Health Association of Yolo County
The Liberty Bell Award from Yolo County Bar Association
The Brinley Award from the City of Davis,
The Golden Rule Award from J. C. Penney
Community Leadership Award, The Woman In History Award from Yolo County in 1997, when I thought I was still too young to be called "history.

But it is not the awards that have meaning for me; they are merely tangible evidence that I didn't give up looking for the good that ill wind did blow. The greatest rewards – the greatest gifts - have been the people I've known and worked with and the experience that has helped me to grow and know happiness.

As Pearl S. Buck once wrote, "Sorrow fully accepted brings its own gifts, for there is alchemy in sorrow. It can be transmuted, which if it does not bring joy, can yet bring happiness." Ira Tanner also describes grief as a gift in his book by a similar title, The Gift of Grief. If we are alive, we cannot escape loss. It is an integral part of living.

The great trick, it seems to me, is to continue to search for the good that loss can bring, for as my grandmother used to tell me,

"'Tis an ill wind, indeed, that blows no good.

The End

Appendix I
Memorial Service for Keith A. Snodgrass
1958-1971
January 6, 1971
Unitarian Church of Davis

Eulogy
By Rev. Robert Senghas

The death of any child who has not reached the fullness of years is always hard to bear; since we grieve not only for the loss of someone close to us, but we grieve also for the lost chance for that child to know the joys which come to us in maturity; and to feel the full flowering of our humanity. In the case of Keith Snodgrass we have an additional burden. When he died at the age of 12, it was already clear that he possessed high qualities and potential. Earlier than for most of us, his personality had crystallized a good bit. He had a style of his own. Many were charmed by his power of persuasion; this means that he must have been highly aware of the needs and feelings of others. He was adventuresome and fun-loving, and loved sports, as befits a boy of spirit; at the same time he was also developing a sense of personal responsibility. He had not long before his death begun a paper route, and he took the responsibility seriously. He had also joined Troop 66 of the Boy Scouts, and was enthusiastic about scouting. Whatever he did, he did with personal style and vitality.

The music in this service is by musicians that meant a lot to Keith; he loved the music of the Beatles and Simon and Garfunkel, and it is significant that much of this music expresses complex feelings and thoughts.

Keith was already developing a sense of who he was, of his selfhood. He had a favorite poster at home, a poster which had on it the words of the American thinker Henry David Thoreau. When he read the words on the poster he remarked to his mother that Thoreau's words described him well. "That's me, Mom," he said. We shall close the service with these words of Thoreau from the poster:

If a man does not keep pace with his companions; perhaps it is because he hears a different drummer. Let him step to the music which he hears, however measured or far away.

Appendix II

Memorial Service for Glen J. Snodgrass
1931-1971
January 8, 1971
Unitarian Church of Davis

Eulogy
By Rev. Robert Senghas

Tonight we pay tribute to an unusual man. The life of Glen Snodgrass was centered on two points: his family and his work. Since there are many who know him in only one of those aspects, it is important that we make both aspects known.

Glen grew up a devoted son. His father died when he was 11 years old, and he helped his mother by working, and worked his way through college. He accepted willingly the responsibilities life lay before him.

He was a complex person. He developed at an early time an ability to chart his own course, and often chose to follow that course in preference to the path of the multitude. He tended to avoid the usual social events and parties. In issues of substance, however, like politics and philosophy, he enjoyed the stimulation of energetic discussions with a few persons, and he would sometimes play "Devil's Advocate" in order to bring out the issues fully. He also liked competitive games, and was an avid reader with a wide range of subjects.

But if he often preferred solitude, it was a caring solitude. He cared deeply for his family and for those with whom he worked, and when he was needed, he was there. He never let his children down.

His caring extended beyond those around him. Many do not know that when he was on the staff of Touro Infirmary in New Orleans, he helped bring about the racial integration of that Infirmary. In 1965 he marched in a public demonstration in New Orleans at the murder of the Unitarian Universalist clergyman James Reeb in Selma, at a time and place when such an act was neither safe nor popular.

Glen was greatly devoted to his work. He helped start the Tumor Institute at Mount Zion Hospital in San Francisco. He needed challenge; he was the kind of man who is a mover in more than one sense, a man who helps establish something and organize it so that it can run routinely, and who then moves on.

Glen was the first man to join Dean Tupper at the beginning of the Medical School here at Davis. Earlier, in 1963, Glen had been the author of the feasibility study for the Medical School here which came to be known as the "Snodgrass Report." This is the study which was submitted to the Regents of the University and endorsed by them in October of 1963. Their endorsement signaled the approval for proceeding with the four-year medical school.

Later when Dean Tupper arrived here, he was so impressed with the far-sightedness of the author of the report that he sought Glen out and finally found him in New Orleans. Glen was first asked to come here for two weeks as a consultant, and then asked to stay; and he did come to stay in April, 1966. The Dean is said that in his judgment the Medical School can be considered a monument to Glen Snodgrass.

Recently, when the University of California needed a ten-year forecast for is state-wide health sciences needs, Glen was given chief responsibility for staff work in the preparation of this forecast. Last fall Glen spent two months in Berkeley working on this plan, and Glen

190

was very much moved by the action of the faculty of the Medical School here, when they endorsed his report unanimously.

Glen was the unusual person who is able both to see the larger outline and goal and also to attend to the small details.

Despite the important responsibility and influence his office gave him, Glen was not ambitious for power or political influence. He used to say that the life of an administrator consists of an "in" drawer, a desk, and an "out" drawer, and that the object was to get the material as fast from the "in" to the "out" drawer, with as short a time as possible on the desk in between.

Glen was not the kind of person who presents one face to his superiors and another to those who work for him. I have spoken to men and women for whom Glen worked and who worked for Glen, and they describe the same man. Here are their words: "the focal point of activities in the office"; "concerned, kind, considerate"; "one of the most devoted and conscientious men – selfless, motivated, inspirational."

There was already an indication that high and creative responsibility was to be forthcoming.

One of the last books read by Glen was The Love Story by Erich Segal. There is a sentence in that book that Glen appreciated, which says, "Love means never having to say you're sorry." Glen believed this, and knowing this, we know that he would prefer those who love him not to submerge themselves in vain regrets for what might have been, but rather to celebrate the great contributions he gave his family, his profession, his colleagues, and to everyone during the short 39 years he was here. As Dean Tupper said, we may take some comfort that he did more in 39 years than many do in a whole lifetime.

And finally, beyond everything else that has been said, there is the absolute testament of the manner of Glen's death. As it was said, "Greater love has no man, than this, that a man lay down his life for his friends." That is how Glen lived, and that is how he died. More than that is not possible for any man, that in death he celebrated the value of life in its ultimate form.

Appendix III

You may know where all of your documents and financial information is, but will your survivor or caregiver? I know that it may have been more difficult for me due to loss of important papers in the fire, but even so, I believe that it is most important for anyone – young or old – to have an organizational system to assure easy access to vital information. When I looked the other day on www.amazon.com, I found many books to help you organize pertinent information.

Information that may be needed: (Where are they located?) If they're in a safety deposit box, where do you keep the key?

Birth Certificate
Citizenship papers
Power of Attorney
Military Discharge papers
Passport
Marriage Certificate
Divorce/Separation Papers (if applicable)
Death Certificate of spouse (if applicable)
Old tax returns
Accountant or Tax Preparer
The title to your car
Property deed
Bank accounts – address, password/pin# for access to Internet
    Checking account
    Savings account
Safe Deposit Box Number, location, and location of keys
Credit Cards and Charge cards – numbers, pin# and passwords, if applicable
Debit Account – Password/pin# or clue for Internet purposes
Investment information, such as name of financial institution, contact information, account numbers, paperwork location, appointed power of attorney, if any, for the following:
Stocks
Bonds
Mutual Funds
Annuities
CD's

401K's
Other investments
Property Deeds and Titles
Mortgages
Leases
Vehicles – Registration, Date of purchase, Pink slip,
Personal property list (I recommend a video of personal property, including art, furniture, jewelry, etc. that should be kept away from property.)
Insurance information, including life, auto, property, liability and fire insurance, disability and long-term care policies: numbers, name of company, location of policies, etc.
Retirement benefits, e.g. Social Security, pension information, Medicare, etc.
Living Will – location of document or who to contact
Last Will and Testament – location of document, date executed
End of life wishes - funeral, burial or cremation, cemetery, plot information, who to contact

And lastly, if as is the case with our current household, many of your financial transactions are done on-line, such as bills being paid electronically and automatically through a program such as Quicken, be sure there is a list of passwords, location, and contacts.

No one knows when an accident or an illness may happen. It's best to be prepared…just in case that ill wind doth blow.

Resources and Support

Grief is a reaction to loss, any loss. We grieve for a wide variety of losses throughout our lives. Bereavement is the way we process grief. A support group and reading about grief and bereavement facilitated the process for me. However, because many of the books in my library and references for support are out of print or out of date, I would recommend the following book, as the authors have done a thorough study of current resources. While it is addressed to those who have experienced loss through sudden death, I believe it useful for any loss and a valuable reference for friends and counselors, as well. It includes a large section on self-help, as well as grief recovery exercises. I agree with these authors who have done their homework when they say, "It is important to do not just to think." If you can get only one book, this is one I would recommend:

I Wasn't Ready to Say Goodbye: Surviving, Coping, and Healing after the Sudden Death of a Loved One **by Brook Noel & Pamela D. Blair, Ph.D., who write from experience. Champion Press, 2000.**

Dougy Center, Portland, Oregon – Wide variety of resources
http://www.dougy.org/grief-resources/

Medic Publishing, Ind., P. O. Box 89, Redmond, WA. 98073-0089 12-page quick and to the point easy-to-read $3.00 pamphlets, including:
- *A Better Ending* – for caregivers
- *Parent's Grief* Help and Understanding After the Death of a Baby
- *Healing a Father's Grief* – for not only the bereaved father, but for the wife and others to give them insight and understanding of the gender differences at this difficult process.
- *Loss: How Children and Teenagers Can Cope with Death and Other Kinds of Loss*

- *Children's Grief* with five sections: baby, preschool, pre-adolescents/adolescents, and young adults.
- *Sibling Grief*
- *Healing Grief*

Guiding Your Child through Grief by James and Mary Ann Emswiler, Bantam, 2000..

Talking About Death: A Dialogue between Parent and Child by Earl A. Grollman, Beacon Press, 1991, explaining the loss of a loved one to a child from preschool to pre-teen.

Straight Talk bout Death for Teenagers: How to Cope With Losing Someone You Love by Earl Grollman, Beacon Press, Boston, Mass. 1993

How it Feels When a Parent Dies by Jill Krementz, Alfred A. Knopf, 1981. These short writings show a range of reactions by 18 young people to the death of a parent. The authors come from many different backgrounds, ages, situations and circumstances, yet they hold one thing in common: they've each lost a parent. Authentic writing. Great for adolescents and adults.

When Bad Things Happen to Good People, Harold Kushner, Avon Books, N. Y. 1988

Learning to Say Good-by When A Parent Dies, E. LeShan, Avon, N. Y. 1978

A Grief Observed by C. S. Lewis. Absolute candor about the agonizing days of his grief after the death of his beloved wife.

The Gift of Grief: Healing the Pain of Everyday Losses by Ira Tanner,Hawthorne Books 1976

The Bereaved Parent by Harriet Sarnoff Schiff, Crown Publishers, 1976

Now That He's Gone: A Financial Therapists Guide to Life After Loss by Barbara Tobocman, Edwards Brothers 2008.
Tobocman offers more than financial advice in this lighthearted look at reorganizing after any kind of personal loss.

It's an Ill Wind, Indeed...that blows no good
A Memoir
By Joan Callaway

For questions and discussion of It's an Ill Wind, Indeed...
http://www.facebook.com/#!/groups/244293938914344/

Grief and color chart graphics – Marilyn Judson; author portrait – Tom Deininger; Cover by Giovanni Gelati.

ALSO BY JOAN CALLAWAY
The Color Connection from a Retailer's Perspective

Website
http://webspace.cal.net/~callaway/tarika/Welcome.html

Made in the USA
Charleston, SC
04 September 2011